# GOD SPEAKS, WOMEN RESPOND

# GOD SPEAKS,
## WOMEN RESPOND

*UCC Women in Ministry Tell Their Stories*

EDITED BY

NANCY PEELER KEPPEL

AND

JEANETTE STOKES

UNITED
CHURCH
PRESS

THIS BOOK IS DEDICATED
TO WOMEN EVERYWHERE WHO
ARE RESPONDING TO GOD
IN WORD AND DEED.

United Church Press, 700 Prospect Avenue East, Cleveland, Ohio 44115
© 2004 by United Church Press
unitedchurchpress.com

All Scripture quotations, unless otherwise indicated, are from the *New Revised
Standard Version Bible*, copyright 1989 by the Division of Christian Education
of the National Council of the Churches of Christ in the U.S.A. In some
instances, the text may have been adapted for inclusivity. Used by permission.

All rights reserved. Published 2004
Printed in the United States of America

09   08   07   06   05   04        5   4   3   2   1

Photo credits:
Jill R. Edens, Photo © Artie Dixon, Chapel Hill, NC, 2003: page 43;
Mary Emma Evans, Photo by Susan Campbell: page 56;
Sallye Hardy, Photo by Tom Alred, Jr.: page 72;
Maria Palmer, Photo © Bruce Clark Photography, Raleigh, NC: page 146;
Diane (Wolff) Snowa, Photo by Richard Boushell, © 2001: page 180

Library of Congress Cataloging-in-Publication Data

God speaks, women respond : UCC women in ministry tell their stories /
    edited by Nancy Peeler Keppel and Jeanette Stokes.
        p. cm.
    ISBN 0-8298-1663-1 (pbk : alk. paper)
    1. Women clergy–Southern States–Biography.  2. United Church of
    Christ–Clergy–Biography.  I. Keppel, Nancy Peeler, 1930-  II. Stokes,
    Jeanette.
BX9886.Z8G63 2004
285.8'34'082—dc22                                        2004052133

# CONTENTS

# Contents

# FOREWORD

YVONNE V. DELK

In First Samuel we encounter a woman with a fervent desire of the heart to bring forth life. The hope that is within her is so pressing that she cannot let it go. And so, she begins a journey of faith against the wind, against the norms of her day, against the cruelty of her husband and the culture in which she was born. At times she feels as if she is all alone—trapped in a place of deep despair with no hope. She cries out to God, praying through tears and disappointment, seeking a word from God. When she possesses a sigh too deep for words, she simply moves her lips. Some think that she is drunk or perhaps demon-possessed when they observe her strange behavior and reflect on her audacious hope that life can come through her closed womb.

Still, somewhere in the depth of her soul, she knows that God has not forgotten her. She believes that God hears her prayers, knows the hope that is within her heart, and that, in due season, God will speak. Therefore, she presses on, believing that there is a way through—a way to move, a way to hope, a way to believe, and she refuses to give up. She pours out her soul to God, believing that God will use her and will speak through her and through the gift of life that she will bear. Her name is Hannah, and she is willing to completely surrender herself to God in order to fulfill the purpose for which she has been called. She believes that life is a gift from God, and when God answers her prayer, she vows not to hoard that life; rather, in gratitude and thanksgiving, she will offer it back to God.

Hannah could be considered a forerunner for the stories of the women that you will encounter in this book. The stories of these sisters in ministry carry a central theme of pressing against the wind to give birth to the call that they received from God. These are women who, like the yeast, continue to rise from the injustices of their past to claim their names, their identities, their authority, and their passion for ministry.

The stories in this book are rooted and connected to women of faith in all times and ages who have responded to the call of God on their lives. The journey has taken us from catacombs to cathedrals and from kitchen tables to communion tables. It has found us struggling to find our way through centuries of conquest, genocide, sexism, and slavery to conversion, repentance, and new history. We have embarked on a journey that will take us from exploitation and oppression to a time of turning, healing, and new direction.

While some of the women in these chapters knew early in their journey that God had called them to preach, others did not have a clue until God's call tracked them down in unexpected ways and places. The paths traveled were not easy, bringing them face to face with the themes of racism, sexism, trivialization, political subordination, domestication by language, imagery, and ecclesiastical traditions. However, God's **Yes** was much louder than the **No**'s around them. Their courage, determination, and ability to hear God speaking provided the strength that allowed them to confront their own demons and the systemic forces that attempted to negate the validity of their call. When facing challenges and obstacles, they refused to give up or give out, but continued to press on in the unshakable belief that the God who had created them would open doors for them that no one could shut. They believed that God's **Yes** was more powerful than the **No**'s of the circumstances in which they had been born, the life experiences that they encountered, or the patriarchal culture of the Bible, church, and society.

I feel deeply connected to these sisters in ministry because their story is connected to my story. As an African American woman in ministry who answered the call more than forty-five years ago, I embarked on a journey that would lead to an unimagined future. However, when I stepped on the campus of Andover Newton Theological School in Newton Center, Massachusetts, in 1961, I wondered how I had arrived at this predominantly white, male seminary. I must have had a temporary moment of insanity to permit Rev. Percel Alston to guide me in this direction.

I was the only African American woman in the class that entered in 1961. Actually there were only thirteen women in that entire class and most of us were religious education majors. If location and place are indicators of how one is valued, it is clear that the seminary did not see us as equal to the men on that campus. The women's dormitory was at the bottom of the hill while everything else—men's dormitories, library, classrooms, cafeteria, administrative buildings—were all at the top of the hill. The men constantly put down some of the courses we took, referring to them as "sandbox" courses as opposed to the "intellectually stimulating" courses that prepared them for ministry. I have to smile as I reflect on the fact that two-thirds of the curriculum was the same for all, while the other third was tailored to one's major. Some of them even had the audacious belief that the real reason we were there was to find husbands.

Throughout my seminary experience and my continuing journey to claim and own my call, I have wrestled with three primary issues. The first has to do with the nature of my identity—who I understand myself to be in relationship to God, community, institution, and broader culture. I am a daughter of the black church, and while the church was clear on its role as it related to racism, it was a sexist environment for women entering ministry. The role of a woman was viewed as being subordinate to that of a man.

As I struggled with my identity, I have to admit that at the beginning of my journey, I did not believe that God had called me into the ordained ministry. I could not imagine being a pastor, preacher, priest, or prophet. The church and culture around me had convinced me that these were roles that God had ordained for men. However, the Holy Spirit has a way of breaking through and breaking us out of the boxes in which we live. I could not live too easily in my male-only box because my own grandmother was an ordained minister in the First United Holy Church of America, Inc., and all around me were images of African American women in church and society claiming their names and their place, moving to music that had not yet been written.

Therefore, as I grew into my understanding of my call, I realized that the call is very personal and specific. By virtue of our confession of faith and our baptism into the household of Jesus Christ, we are called to be disciples. I joined the church when I was only eight years old. On that day, when I walked the aisle of Macedonia UCC in Norfolk, Virginia, and surrendered my life to Jesus Christ, a call was placed on my life. It is a call that I continue to wrestle with every day.

Isaiah 43 is a reminder that God had not only called me but also called me by my name. The call comes in the context of our histories, our experiences, our pain, our joy. The call is not about being God's elite or God's favorite or God's pampered people. To the contrary, it is about naming and claiming. It is about being claimed by God for God's purposes. It is about obedience and faithfulness. It is about the cost and the joy of discipleship. To be called by name is to be invited into a new way of being and doing. The call is not limited to gender, race, or class; rather, it is about surrendering one's life to God, and, in the surrender, to be confronted, broken, and molded again so that one can live as God's disciple in church and society.

The second issue focused on the nature of authority. The question I wrestled with was how to own and claim my authority while being educated in a predominantly white, male seminary. When after graduation, I found myself serving in institutions where the center of power was also white and male, I had to keep in focus the question "What is it that informs you of who you are in ways from which you are not free to walk?" What I see and affirm has, in large part, been determined by the path that I have traveled. My mother's words are deep within me— "no matter where life takes you, Yvonne, always remember who you are and whose you are."

My faith meanings have been filtered through my life experiences. As I entered the halls of Andover Newton Theological School, I had to trust what I knew to be true as an African American woman growing up in a racist, sexist, class-structured society. I had to filter the experience and the vision of the gospel of Jesus Christ through my psyche, my life, and my wounds. The insights into and experience of Jesus Christ would free me to live the life of a woman that was created in God's image and would provide me with a road map for living and creating the world that God intends. Throughout my journey, black theology, liberation theology, and women's theology have been significant in helping me to claim my authority and my call. I now know the meaning of the African proverb "It does not matter what they call you, it is what you answer to that matters."

One's authority is rooted in having a standing ground from which to answer "yes" and "no." I had found my ground in that which had allowed me to survive, to function, to maintain some degree of sanity and hope. It was this ground that kept me pressing on, many times against the wind. At a deeper level, my authority was inextricably bound to how I answered the questions of who God is, who I am in relationship to this God, and what this God requires of me.

The third issue had to do with the nature of my call. What did God want me to do and where would I do it? I will always remember the look of total disbelief when I shared the news with my sociology professor, Dr. Blue, that upon graduation from college, I would attend a seminary rather than pursue a master's degree in sociology. Dr. Blue had mentored me for a career in sociology and had arranged for me to receive a full-time scholarship at the Atlanta University School of Social Work to pursue a master's degree in sociology. "What do you plan to do when you leave seminary?" he asked. At that moment, I knew that I did not have an answer. I knew that I wanted to return to my southern soil and to the black church to serve. However, most of the black churches in the Southern Conference of the United Church of Christ were struggling to pay the meager salaries paid to the male minister. It was incomprehensible that they would pay the salary of a director of religious education—especially when they could get volunteers to do the Christian education task of the church. With race and racism on the table, employment within a white church was out of the question.

The question of call continued to be a major wrestling point. I had entered seminary prepared to be trained as a director of Christian education. However, this was simply my entry place; God would take me further than I had imagined! Ten years after graduating from seminary, God was still speaking, and I knew that I was ready to move from the position of a commissioned worker in the field of Christian education into ordained ministry. God's call crosses all the traditional boundaries that we create. I had to surrender my past insecurities and fears in order to offer an unconditional **Yes** to the call that would take me out of my comfort zone and would find me breaking through walls and barriers while proclaiming and witnessing to the gospel of Jesus Christ.

I have never served as a pastor of a church but I have been a pastor to many. I have served the church as an educator, a preacher, a priest, and a prophet. I have traveled as an ordained minister to many places throughout the globe lifting up a vision of a Just Peace World—the world I believe that God intends. I have been described as a spiritual preacher, a committed activist, a soul on fire. My call did not take me to the place that I expected; rather, it took me along an amazing path of witness and proclamation. The call does not respect the rules of homogeneity and comfortable security. The call is to the whole people for the whole ministry of God wherever the Spirit leads.

The common stream that I share with the other women in this book is that we are women who found ourselves, at some point in our ministry, in the southern region of the United States. This soil has brought us face to face with racism, sexism, classism, homophobia, the Bible belt, and fundamentalism. We are also women who celebrate our existence in the free space of a denomination that has ordained women since 1853. While the United Church of Christ is still in the state of becoming what God intends for it to be, it seeks to create a church that is truly receptive of the gifts of women. Finally, I share the joy of being a sister in this family of women who continues to create a path that affirms God's **Yes** for our lives in spite of and because of the **No's** that we encounter each day. We started from different places, function in different ways and in different ministries, and yet, these streams continue to weave common themes throughout our stories.

This book is our living record. Our stories must be told because they represent the "herstory" of the paths that we have traveled. Our stories must be told because somebody needs to know our names. Our stories must be told because they provide authority and encouragement for those who need to hear God speaking in their wilderness experience and in those places they call home.

In *My Soul is a Witness,* Donna Marimba Richards reminds us that each of our stories in some way connects to the others thereby forming a continuing vibrant circle of "herstory."

> We would form a circle, each touching those next to us to physically express our spiritual closeness. We "testified," speaking on the day's or the week's experiences. We shared the pain of those experiences and received from the group affirmations of our experiences as suffering beings. As we "lay down our burdens," we became lighter. As we testified and listened to others testify, we began to understand ourselves as communal beings, no longer the "individuals" that the system tried to make us. . . . We sang and moved until we were able to experience totally the spirit within us. . . . We became again a community.[1]

God is speaking today as clearly as when God spoke to Hannah and to the women in this book. Their testimonies of faith and courage in the midst of challenges and obstacles provide hope and encouragement. Each writer in her own way has shared out of her pain and her joy while keeping the faith and pressing on to make a difference. The stories remind us that the circle remains unbroken. Each writer received faith and encouragement from those who came before, and each writer, in return, offers the same to those who will come after.

1. Gloria Wade-Gayles, ed., *My Soul is a Witness: African-American Women's Spirituality,* (Boston: Beacon Press, 1995), 96.

# PREFACE

NANCY PEELER KEPPEL

Supporting and encouraging women in ministry has long been a ministry for me. I have had the privilege of knowing and working with many UCC clergywomen and commissioned ministers since 1974 when I initiated the Southern Conference Task Force on Women in Church and Society. On March 7, 2002, my 72nd birthday, I thought of a way to honor them and sent a letter to sixteen women inviting them to tell their stories of God's call, their preparation for ministry, and the different forms that ministry has taken. I told them that their essays would become a book. I wrote, "Each chapter will be approximately ten pages. The stories can include anything that makes them unique, challenging, and inspirational. In an appendix we may put sermons, essays, articles, poems, or whatever else you would like to add."

Months later I realized that I had started a project that I could not possibly finish alone. My only experience as an editor was in high school when I edited the annual because no one else would do it. Fortunately, I had known Jeanette Stokes and her excellent work as

director of the Resource Center for Women and Ministry in the South for over twenty-five years. I asked her to take on this project as editor, which she graciously and enthusiastically did. We then enlisted Mary Jo Carledgehayes as consultant and editor. Her professional experience and knowledge were immensely helpful.

Many of the original sixteen ministers responded positively, some had valid reasons not to participate, and more ministers were added later. I was encouraged to write my story, which I hesitated to do at first since I am not ordained. Then I realized that it could serve as a bridge to a book of stories by laypeople in ministry.

God is still speaking. These ministers are living proof. It has been my great privilege to compile their stories.

# ACKNOWLEDGMENTS

JEANETTE STOKES

When I created the Resource Center for Women and Ministry in the South (RCWMS) in 1977, I wanted to support and encourage women in and entering ministry. One of the very first things RCWMS ever did was to send out information about the 125th anniversary of the ordination of Antoinette Brown Blackwell. I have been fascinated by this united and uniting denomination ever since.

Since I am a Presbyterian clergywoman, it has taken a number of people to teach me about the United Church of Christ. In the late 1970s, John Kernodle, an attorney and a UCC minister, introduced me to Congregational United Church of Christ in Greensboro, North Carolina. His mother, Esther Kernodle, inspired me with stories of women in the United Church of Christ and in Church Women United. Carol Bernard Snyder took me to a couple of national UCC women's gatherings, where I met Nancy Peeler Keppel. At one of these events, Barbara Brown Zikmund gave a slide lecture about the history of women in the United Church of Christ. I returned to North Carolina and created a slide lecture about the history of women in the Southern Conference. I am grateful to Nancy for coaxing me into co-editing this collection and taking another look at women in the United Church of Christ.

Nancy Peeler Keppel and I are grateful to Mary Cartledgehayes, Margie Hattori, and Addie Luther for their encouragement and editing; to Georgann Eubanks for brilliantly producing Mary Evans' CD, *Happy with Jesus Alone;* and to Madrid Tramble at Resource Design and Production Services for turning our manuscript into an actual book.

# INTRODUCTION

JEANETTE STOKES

The United Church of Christ describes itself as a united and uniting denomination. Several streams belonging generally to the Reformed branch of Protestantism came together to form the United Church of Christ. The Congregational Church and the Christian Church merged in 1931 to form the Congregational Christian Church. The Evangelical Synod of North America and the Reformed Church in the United States merged in 1934 to form the Evangelical and Reformed Church. Then in 1957 those two bodies joined to form the United Church of Christ.

While women have been serving as ministers of Jesus Christ since the women appeared at the tomb on that first Easter morning, they have served as ordained ministers in the United States for only about 150 years. The United Church of Christ claims the first of these. Antoinette Brown (later Blackwell) was ordained on September 15, 1853, in the Congregational Church of South Butler, New York, where she was serving as the pastor.

When a new regional body, the Southern Conference of the United Church of Christ, was formed in 1965, three regional bodies came together: the Southern Synod of the Evangelical and Reformed Church; the Southern Convention of the Congregational Christian Church; and the Convention of the South of the Congregational Christian Church, the historically African American churches among Congregational Christians.

The Southern Conference contains a remarkable diversity of Christians in terms of race, class, urban and rural, theological perspectives, and political persuasions. The Eastern North Carolina Association, for example, is roughly half black and half white, with the majority of its churches in small towns or rural settings.

The United Church of Christ embodies the spirit of Christian unity by welcoming members from all over Christendom. Because of its unique history of accepting women's leadership, the United Church of Christ has attracted women seeking a place to use their gifts for ministry. Some of the women represented in *God Speaks, Women Respond* grew up in other denominations: Methodist, Presbyterian, Lutheran, Baptist, and Roman Catholic. The numbers of active clergywomen remained small until the 1970s when women entered graduate and professional schools, including Protestant seminaries, in larger numbers than ever before. As a result, the numbers of clergywomen grew rapidly. While the United Church of Christ is completely open to and supportive of women in ministry, the reality on the ground in the South has been that many clergywomen have had a hard time finding a good fit.

The writers in this volume demonstrate the richness that comes from the variety within the household of faith and among women in ministry. Here you will meet pastors, prophets, counselors, and activists, many of whom have overcome formidable obstacles to live out their calling. One, a Hispanic pastor, built a ministry from the ground up for the Hispanic community in her town. Another, now in her eighties, continues a vibrant ministry among the poor. As a child, one woman preached from a tree stump by a creek to a congregation of wooden bobbins from the cotton mill. Another was told she would make a better businesswoman than preacher. One is a copastor with her husband in a university town; another drives over a hundred miles to serve a tiny congregation. These women write honestly and forthrightly about their challenges. It is inspiring to watch as God shapes their lives around those obstacles. These are lives of action, lived as prayer without ceasing.

The lives of the women in this book demonstrate that if we keep listening and responding, God will open a way. It won't always be the way we expected, but it will be the way to meaningful relationship with God and one another and to lives of service in the church and the world. God is still speaking. These faithful women continue to respond to God's call.

When we began gathering the essays in this collection, the Eastern North Carolina Association was in the midst of a painful disagreement over whether to admit North Raleigh United Church. North Raleigh was a new congregation that was publicly supportive of the ministry and membership of gay, lesbian, bisexual, and transgendered people. Three years later, as we were finishing the collection, the Association voted to receive North Raleigh. In a sermon at a service held to celebrate the reception of the new church, John Thomas, the General Minister and President of the United Church of Christ, said

> In the midst of a deeply contested time in the life of the early church in which competing views threatened to divide Christians from each other, Paul lifts our sights from human judgments, narrow as they often are, to the generosity of God, reminding his listeners and us that it is God's generosity, not our own pedigree or behavior, our own certainty over matters of theological truth, that is the source of our hope and our salvation. The generosity of God has no limits; it is for everyone. Everyone.

# ON THE USEFULNESS OF WORDS

ROBIN J. TOWNSLEY ARCUS

Covers cast colors before my youthful eyes. As a child, I never saw as many books in one place as in my father's study, except perhaps in the town library. My father was a minister. In the church he served, he had a study that was built with one entire wall of shelves reaching from floor to ceiling. It was impressive to see such a collection of books filling every possible space and surface. It never occurred to me to ask if he had actually read them. Whether or not, books were the tools of his trade, obvious even to a casual observer. Whereas our basement housed his carpenter's saw and workbench, upstairs, at church, his study was always full of books.

I was not a reader, but that is not why I did not consider my father's profession for myself. I believe it was because I wasn't a boy. I have a brother, Tom. It would not have been a stretch to imagine him taking up the cloth. Tom was clever, thoughtful. Tom was a reader. Professional ministry must have occurred to him. After all, doesn't every boy try on his father's mantle, at least in his own mind?

From the outsider's view ministry must have appeared a desirable position. It is certainly clean work. Our congregation was made up of farmers, tradesmen, and a few merchants. Those not actively farming were keenly aware to be only a half step off the farm, what with the pervasive smell of manure and some family member still toiling in the soil. More than a few of our church members were missing digits from their hands. Thus, we never lost our respect for the hard, backbreaking, cyclical labor involved. My father's hands remained whole and smooth, but I think some days he might have traded in his pressed shirts and bank of books for a go in the dirt, especially after a monthly Consistory meeting. We kids were sheltered from the specifics, though there were bound to be mutterings and sour faces from our parents, usually at the Sunday dinner table; sometimes it was over the number in attendance that morning. So, I was not unaware of the difficulties of ministry. It just simply never crossed my mind that I should experience them firsthand.

I never much wanted to spend time in church. My father relished the church. He especially loved church architecture, requiring us to stop and try the door at every little country parish along our traveling way. Living in rural Pennsylvania, he found lots and lots of doors. Provided my father could get inside, which was still possible in the 1960s, he would take a long look around, and then without fail, he would mount the stairs to the pulpit. It was as though he was trying it on for size, like a pair of shoes or trousers. Having finished his silent evaluation, we would all file out, with me leading the pack.

In 1978, my father became terminally ill. My mother held vigil at my father's bedside while I smoked cigarettes, gossiped with my friends, and forgot the way to the hospital. I was fifteen and unaccustomed to mature behavior.

My father's being lowered into the ground did nothing for my faith. Funeral directors don't let you stay and watch, so you're left only to your dreams and imagination to view the awful descent. "Say all you want about Easter; my father is dead." And burial, while it is handy in providing a place, a marker for a life once lived, I often wanted to take a flashlight and shovel to see for myself. I have a friend whose eight-year-old daughter just buried her first guinea pig. They chose a shoebox and a place in the backyard. This is Heidi's first experience with death. Bless her soul, she wanted to dig him up after three days.

Who hasn't shared these feelings—the absolute urge to plunge hands into dirt—to scratch desperately at loose soil for resigned confirmation, yes, the box is still there. But think what that does to one's faith. Thank God, Jesus' tomb was empty, but none of these theological precepts was in my awareness. I was set on boys and college, and in that particular order. Therefore, I rarely again wanted to go to church.

Maturity came, as it often does, when I was alone without my family. After college, I moved to Arizona, a long geographical and psychological leap from home. Nothing of the landscape proved familiar, and while I often rolled down my window in traffic to announce to someone with a Pennsylvania license plate, "I'm from Pennsylvania too!" I rarely received more than feigned interest. In Phoenix, everyone was from somewhere else.

In search of familiar land on which to stand, I took myself to church. I was raised in the United Church of Christ; I would visit a UCC congregation. The distinct lines that formed the denomination were lost on me. I was born in 1962, five years after the creation of the consolidated United Church of Christ. To ask if a church was from the Evangelical and Reformed tradition did not occur to me. Were not those differences ironed out? I knew that not every UCC congregation followed the lengthy preparatory service the Sunday before Holy Communion (still hinting of German). I had been in churches where little individual communion cups were dispensed from the front rather than doled out pewside. I gathered there would be differences. What I was looking for were the similarities.

As I entered Desert Palm UCC, I saw a large banner with the United Church of Christ logo, a cross crowned at its top and grounded in a globe. I had seen that symbol so often in my father's study. Like a lost soul feels upon reaching home, my breast swelled with gratitude and pride. Welcomed signs were everywhere, men in suits handing out bulletins, coiffed women in flowered church dresses. And the music; I could hear the sounds of an organist offering a prelude, helping the worshipers separate themselves from the ordinary drone of other days.

I attended worship services at Desert Palm UCC long enough at least to have my faith restored, though what I really experienced was having time ordered again. As happens when following liturgy and the church year, time began to have purpose and meaning, never mind that in Arizona you never put away your shirtsleeves. Or perhaps *because* in the desert you never wear wool, some other division of time becomes acutely necessary. In the church, regardless of the sun, ordinary time turns to Advent, turns to Christmas, to Epiphany, to Lent, to Easter, to Pentecost.

And then I moved to the Carolinas, first to South Carolina where I looked in the phone book for a UCC congregation. There was only one in all of Columbia, the capital city. It turned out to be a cluster of eight people who were struggling to create a UCC identity and call their first pastor. They met in the Sunday school chapel of a large Lutheran church. Typical of such spaces there was a simple lectern, a miniature altar and cross, and an old electronic organ stuck in the corner. These had been enough to serve the purpose. And so when the group learned that I had taken piano lessons, they christened me the church organist, never mind I had no facility with my feet. But that role served to galvanize my faith, or at least gave me reason for weekly attendance. I took my charge seriously and prepared music for every Sunday.

With the promise of support from the UCC Southeast Conference and the National church, our little congregation was permitted to call a pastor. We ended up asking a female minister not because she was a woman but because she would come. We were such an odd bunch, most everyone in the group having some ties to ministry—chaplain, social worker, minister in training, retired from ministry. It was they who urged me to consider seminary. They said, "You're a thoughtful Christian person. Take some classes." I later realized we point people in our own familiar directions.

The Lutheran seminary was not far down the road. At night, I took two courses and then supposed all of seminary would be as exciting and affirming. It might have been useful to have studied under different professors (both classes were taught by the same person). My instructor, Mary Havens, was a new star at Lutheran Theological Southern Seminary. Thus, between our new pastor and Mary Havens, the light finally dawned on me: women could be ministers too!

At twenty-six, after working in business since college, I left my company car and expense account, snipped my American Express card, and enrolled at Duke Divinity School in Durham, North Carolina. I chose Duke largely because I could afford the housing. Having already lived on my own, I couldn't fathom returning to the cooperative living arrangements necessary at Pacific School of Religion or Andover-Newton. In Durham, for $270 a month, I could lease a private apartment.

That Duke was not a United Church of Christ school initially seemed not to bother me. After the first week of classes, I was more worried about the depth of instruction and level of academic expectation, and that I was so short (or the chairs so tall) that I could sit and swing my legs like a child. These served not to engender confidence. Nor the D minus I achieved on my first church history paper: "Don't tell me what *you* think. Tell me what *Augustine* thinks!"

Leaving Duke crossed my mind perhaps no more than sixteen times a day, but I stuck it out and in the process found comfort from my small set of UCC friends. Oh, I had Methodist friends, but in that United Methodist environment eventually the United Church of Christ in me called out for identity. I was more determined than ever to be United Church of Christ.

The UCC student-in-care system paired me with a pastor mentor, Cally Rogers-Witte, the copastor of Community United Church in Raleigh. Her investment in social action served as testimony to faith in action. While I did not stand shoulder to shoulder with her at execution vigils or at peace rallies, I imagined her at every place in need of Christian witness. She was a busy person, mobilizing people to fuller expressions of faith. Someone once told me Cally uses the time at stoplights to pray. This seemed a realist's approach to ministry. I was Pennsylvania German enough to understand that.

In Durham, Pilgrim United Church of Christ became my church home. Evidence of ministry was everywhere—community involvement, opportunities to serve, special offerings, meaningful worship. I joined the church choir, which was not a bad choice. Under the direction of Lois Strother, I learned the wonders of sacred music. The tide of contemporary Christian music had been mounting, but not at Pilgrim, and for good reason. Contemporary lyrics fell lamely next to the poetry of the ages. And where the English language failed there was always Latin. Deeper still was the music itself, expressing meaning beyond words. Lois explained that music could be written in the form of the cross, the four notes A, D, B-flat, C-sharp in succession suggesting the four points of the cross. Mozart in his *Requiem* Mass uses this formula in the opening and closing movements. Such an application was not new in Mozart's day, for J. S. Bach and even his predecessors utilized this theologically rich design.

Then I met my husband who, as an organist and music scholar, further introduced me to theology in music. He taught me to be alert to the appearance of threes in music, as references to the Trinity, or the three days from Good Friday to Easter. Three also represents perfection. Early music's practice of using triple meter (three beats to the measure) suggests perfection and when the rhythm of three (perfect) is juxtaposed against two (imperfect) we have demonstrated that when the perfect comes the imperfect will pass away.

Yet another window of meaning was flung wide as I came to understand the riveting and intelligent text painting composers use. Handel, for one, employs much of this throughout *Messiah*, significance that would pass us by without careful examination. In the opening movement "Comfort Ye," we actually *hear* the mountains through the rise and fall of the music. The fury of the bass solo provides the exact right expression in "Why Do the Nations So Furiously Rage Together?" How appropriate that the soprano soloist should sing of the discovery of the empty tomb in "I Know That My Redeemer Liveth." Making these and other musical discoveries brought me deeper into the realm of the sacred.

And then I attended our Southern Conference and Eastern North Carolina Association meetings. There we gathered with our African American colleagues and other people whose emphasis in worship was startlingly different. In order to worship together we had "blended services." In these, we straddled our highly divergent paths to praising God. By my view, the worship planners seemed to dispense with liturgy's centering hold, replacing it with emotional appeal. One need not know of historical practice or purpose, or theological significance; the worshiper was free simply to experience the pleasant in-breaking spirit of God.

Here, the fabric of my Evangelical and Reformed background was stretched and in plenty of places torn. It was true I could learn to hold faith a little closer to my heart rather than always choosing the well-traveled avenue through my head. However, in time, I decided it was a more loving and suitable choice for me to worship God as befits my manner.

I had this confirmed by an African American woman who, like me, was attending a UCC national event in Cleveland. Following a forum, we two women found ourselves discussing the lecture, as well as styles of worship. I risked confessing to her that I had tired of swaying and of praise music, common in so many black churches. I said I kept to a schedule and resented the interminable length of the services and my need to pack a lunch because they go so long.

She laughed and told me I did not need to find black church any more interesting than I did. I told her I secretly feared I was a racist. She turned and looked me squarely in the eye and said, "God wants you to show your praise the very best way you know how."

In May 1991, I married my organist husband, David Arcus. I also finished Duke Divinity School. I had no prospects of church employment, while my Methodist friends were all off to their church appointments. So I wrote my first profile and began its circulation. During this time, I was invited to serve on the Southern Conference Peace and Justice Committee, and given my spacious schedule, I also elected to join the NC Council of Churches Peace and Security Commission.

In January 1992, while my husband and I were attending a sacred music conference in Arizona, I received a literal call in the night. An associate pastor from North Carolina remembered my internship with her church while I was still in seminary. She had tracked me down in Tempe, and overlooking the time difference, her call woke me from sleep. Would I consider returning, specifically to do youth and senior adult ministry? Pinching myself awake, I wondered, *So this is how it works, then?*

My first position in ministry was as a UCC parish associate minister. My duties were to be covered in ten hours of work per week, which I immediately found to be hopelessly limiting if I wanted to build lasting relationships and develop effective programs at the church. I was also invited to preach once a month. Given that it takes at least twenty hours for me to prepare a sermon, I was vastly exceeding the timecard I was supposed to be punching. Yet, I labored on, with fickle youth and fascinating elders. To be among them was my best blessing, though I didn't always see it that way, not amidst schlepping stuff around and placing countless calls for help from busy parents.

I was grateful finally to be put to work, even if the commute was long, as were the hours I lavished on the church. Unfortunately, the academic training I received hardly prepared me for the interpersonal problems that emerged. Then came the new senior minister. He viewed me as a "weak link in the system," presumably because my youth programs did not match with his plans. It was also true that members had formed an attachment to me, which he viewed as a threat to his beginning ministry. Lucky for him my original agreement was to work only for eighteen months to bridge the transition from pastor to pastor. When the end of my contract came, it was time for me to go.

But that first position raised the stakes for my identity as a minister because having a church call provided the one requisite needed to seek ordination. Thus, while serving at that first church, on Pentecost 1992, I was ordained into the ministry. My relatives came from Pennsylvania. My mother cried. The cake I had ordered from Winn-Dixie had a peculiar appearance. I had mentioned at the bakery counter that I was hoping for a decorative motif of Pentecost flames and tongues. The result was an odd coloration of yellow and red icing streaking across the top, with tongues lapping downward. I should have recognized its oddness as a prophetic sign of my less than conventional ministry to come.

In 1994, I learned of a small Christian Church with a pulpit vacancy. I was invited simply to "come and preach for a Sunday." They were a congregation of no more than twenty members and so their worship services were held only every other week. After my first service, I was asked to come back the next time. I returned, and after that occasion I was invited one more time, and then again. Each time I was asked to return only after I had been with them that particular week. On this went for several months.

In time I wrote a letter to the members of the church asking if they would consider calling me as their pastor. They need not pay me more, or even call me *the minister. Interim* would do, if anything more seemed too confining. We were reaching the end of December and my hope was to start us fresh for the calendar year.

There was no move on their part. Then an estranged wife died, and after that a young son. I was not invited to participate in the funeral services, but I was asked to return in January for the first worship service of the month. I went in January, and then they asked me to come back for the third Sunday. I wrote another letter and suggested if they wanted to call me as a pastor, interim or otherwise, they needed to say so, but I was not in a position to continue operating this way. I said I would come the third Sunday in January as my final Sunday unless I heard otherwise. When I heard nothing, I sadly packed my proverbial kit and called it over. They were somehow surprised when I didn't show up the fifth Sunday in January.

In 1996, I learned of an opening at another UCC church. By this time, I was fully aware that women were not being hired through conventional practices, and thus, serving as a temporary supply pastor for a church where I might be considered for hire. They were shopping and, frankly, so was I. After several consecutive Sundays together, the church took a vote, and I was unanimously approved to become their minister. Their former pastor had left after some eight years of service, not over any apparent disagreement but to apply himself to his full-time work. Ministry at this church paid little, even though that little was hard earned on both ends.

I was warned by veteran ministers not to make waves in a new situation. So I lived with the congregation's obvious displays of patriotism, exclusive language, even the "kindly" remarks about a pastor in a skirt. What I could not abide was their inward focus and lack of participation in wider church events. I encouraged them to come to Conference and Association activities. We joined a community Ash Wednesday service. We even worshiped with the Baptists on one occasion, though this was nothing monumental. My congregation was closer in affinity to the Baptist church than any other denomination. Slowly, I reactivated the missions committee. We had several members quite versed in *PTL*'s televised needs of the world, could we not build on that? I told them Billy Graham's son was launching a shoebox campaign for children in need. Church World Service gave us instructions for making school kits for kids. In the second year, if not smoothly, we were at least running along.

Then it happened. A wedding. From the congregation one of the daughters of the church announced she was getting married. There are those who scoff at trying to teach anything to a young couple in love, but I had set a policy to meet at least four times in advance of any marriage ceremony.

This particular pair seemed mostly on track, though clearly there were parental issues to be worked out. Young as they were, eighteen and nineteen, the bride was still living at home. She was unhappy about her mother's interference in her wedding choices. To me her complaints seemed the usual arguments surrounding these types of affairs. However, I should never for a moment have thought *I* would escape the same scrutiny the bride's mother was issuing. When it came to the wedding service, I wrongly reasoned that the minister would be in charge.

In our final session of counseling, the bride and groom met with me to go over the service. We were making final decisions on scripture, and other particularities. I asked if the bride's father would be escorting her down the aisle. "Yes," she answered. "I thought my daddy should give me away."

This precipitated from me a discussion of modern thinking that women are no longer viewed as property. Could we come up with some other method here or use the worship book's words to include mother *and* father? Or better still (I was out on a limb now), we could include words of support from the entire family!

The two seemed happy enough. It would be up to me to construct such a presentation. So I drafted the bulletin complete with their choice of scripture, music, vows, and the fated family promises. And here is where I learned a very valuable lesson. The minister should always oversee the printing of the wedding program. The bride's mother, taking charge of this task, looked over the order of service and solidly announced, "If this is the kind of wedding you want, I'm not paying for any part of it!" A panicked bride sobbed this to me over a pay telephone three days before her wedding. The problems included the responsive psalm—why involve the guests?—and the manner of presenting the bride.

I called an emergency meeting of the bride and groom. I invited them to tell me what they thought of the service as I had outlined it. Did they want to make any changes? They liked it as it was. I told them we next had to call a meeting of the five of us, myself, them, and the bride's parents. I then warned, "This will be your first proving ground. It will set the stage for your identity as a couple. In this meeting, I will allow your parents to have their say, but in the end, I will turn and ask you what *you* want. And know this, I will abide by your answer. It is, after all, your wedding." This seemed the only plausible solution and so I assured them that while this would not be easy, they could count on me.

The next evening I nervously invited the parents and couple into my tiny church study. We sat. I opened with my concern for everyone and the hope that we could achieve a workable arrangement. I asked the parents to air their concerns. They did. I acknowledged these. I explained the meaning behind the service liturgy and why we were involving the families and congregation. I asked if the parents had any other worries. They said no. I turned to the couple at that critical moment and asked, "As the bride and groom, what would *you* like for your service?" And the bride gushed forth, *"Whatever my parents want!"*

On the wedding day, I showed up early to witness church fixtures being carried out of the church and flower trellises being carried in. Furniture I didn't even suppose could be lifted was being moved from the sanctuary. I stood bewildered as pews came out and the three ministers' chairs. When I saw them with the pulpit, I rushed toward them like a mad woman. The helpers explained they were under instruction from the bride's mother. I bade them to return the pulpit and not to consider moving it under order from me. A shot had been fired. A war was on.

Somehow, the wedding happened. Somehow, we got through it. Somehow, I continued showing up to church, but it was evident that the members were abuzz with the wedding. The bride's mother launched an underground campaign to subvert my authority and ideas. The missions we had been undertaking were stalled. People were suddenly not sure if they liked how I had the candles lit on Sunday morning or my choice of hymns or the inclusion of the Lord's Prayer. What was once a tepid congregation turned into an engaged one. Perhaps I should have parlayed their attention into a demonstration of ministerial conviction. However, over time I feared I would have been inviting a nasty split in the congregation. My most loyal and visible parishioners knew what was happening. I bid them please to tell the mother to knock it off. They shyly replied, "Ministers come and ministers go, but we will always be here." Defeated, my prayers turned to "God, help me leave."

Since 1997, I have had only one serious interview for a church position. In that particular case, the search committee and I saw we were not well-suited and therefore no offer was made. And so my profile continues to circulate. Perhaps because I am limited by staying close to Durham, I am not frequently called. However, much has happened in this hardly fallow time.

Throughout the 1990s I was part of a team giving instruction on the UCC program *Created in God's Image (CIGI)*. CIGI is a twelve-week program on human sexuality and is designed to provide a context for Christian people to talk about this tender topic, personally and as an issue of society.

In our efforts to train churches in the use of the CIGI program, I was fortunate to work with Nancy Peeler Keppel, a lay minister, and the idea person behind this book. Nancy, along with her pastor from Community UCC, Dave Barber, and I conducted many training workshops. We shuttled across North Carolina and Virginia to meet with eager groups as well as people who had different agendas. We spent the better part of ten years on behalf of the denomination aiding the advancement of this timely program.

Being free of pastoral duties since 1997 has also allowed me to apply myself to a long desired project—the search for my biological family. My minister father and mother had adopted me when I was three months old. Typical of such arrangements in the 1960s, little information was shared, nothing beyond the name "Baby Carol" and that I had come from a family in an area near where my adopted parents once lived. This proximity gave the adoption agency ample reason to keep quiet any details that might help piece together the true story.

Without a pulpit ministry, I had additional time to dwell on these matters. Thus, I set out to finish what I actually began in 1988 prior to seminary—a search for my biological family. Blessed by the help and love of my adopted mother, I worked to locate the people who were biologically responsible for making me. I have since met some of my relatives and have written extensively about that journey.

I have also written commentary for public radio and helped develop literature for nonprofit organizations. I currently work for a local magazine, *The Urban Hiker,* which publishes the stories of people in our community.

I have served as supply minister to churches of various denominations. I am frequently asked at Duke University Chapel to serve as liturgist for their services and to preside over Holy Communion. The writing of sermons and liturgy seems to me an act of creation, sitting at the desk, reading the lectionary, studying, praying. Within this sacred process of construction, I have discovered the value and critical nature of words.

Ministers trade in words. After all, what else do we have? Faith is formed through words. Words are not simply strung-together letters. "In the beginning was the Word." It turns out those books lining my father's shelves served a purpose. They revealed and translated this One from whom all things were made.

As ministers, we seek to translate and construct language to some meaningful end. As a master mason labors to build a strong wall, we attempt to craft religious language that is equally well engineered, to stand in the most difficult of storms.

Sunday by Sunday, ministers are practitioners of words; we are translators, poets. We are guardians of *the Word.* Yet, not only *the Word:* we are also preservationists of the entire length of Christian history, the historical practices of the church, and the liturgy, which forms us week by blessed week. These precious icons have descended through the ages to pass into and through our hands. Their course has been entrusted to us by all the earlier generations. It is true that we are simple contemporary vessels, but we must remember that all were, and all but one, were only human. Ministers are assigned charge of these words, words that bear grand and sobering responsibility: to baptize, to confirm, to comfort, to convict, to bury, to absolve, and to heal. Therefore, come what may for my own pulpit ministry, I pray for all who minister. Let us beware these treasures we hold, rise to their high standard, and share them among the nations and races as worthy conduits of a crowning faith.

## O Word of God Incarnate

O Word of God incarnate,
O Wisdom from on high,
O Truth unchanged, unchanging,
O Light of our dark sky:
We praise Thee for the radiance
That from the hallowed page,
A lantern to our footsteps,
Shines on from age to age.

The Church from Thee, her Master,
Received the gift divine,
And still that light she lifteth
O'er all the earth to shine.
It is the sacred casket,
Where gems of truth are stored;
It is the heaven-drawn picture
Of Thee, the living Word.

It floateth like a banner
Before God's host unfurled;
It shineth like a beacon
Above the darkling world.
It is the chart and compass
That o'er life's surging sea,
'Mid mists and rocks and quicksands,
Still guides, O Christ, to Thee.

O make Thy Church, dear Saviour,
A lamp of purest gold,
To bear before the nations

Thy true light as of old.
O teach Thy wandering pilgrims
By this their path to trace,
Till, clouds and darkness ended,
They see Thee face to face.

*(Hymn text by William W. How, 1823–1897)*

*Soli Deo gloria!*

# PASTORAL PRAYER

### Duke University Chapel, June 23, 2002

⊞

## ROBIN J. TOWNSLEY ARCUS

Almighty God, the pass of your hand unfurled the heavens and spread the planets across the sky. You made the earth to belong to you, with nature as your handmaid. The sun is now plump in her season and rules in robust delight. And we savor your summer fruits.

God, it is a pleasure to be governed by your light, fair to taste your sweetness. Let not this day die without our giving thanks for the buds you bring to blossom, nor for the fish who frolic in the sea. For all you give is good, liberal in portion, and well-intended. Praise be to you, God of all creation.

Yet, O God, we fail to aportion your gifts fairly. We impute motives of malice and declare judgment on our neighbors. We decide that those who go without are guilty of greater sin. Pry open our miserly hands and flood our parched hearts that your blessing may stream through us, to others, from your fountains of joy and plenty.

We confess we are charmed by temptations, and waste our time on love's infinite imitations. We fear evil, which can destroy our bodies and souls, but we cannot sever our attachments. Whisper to us the remedy, this time to believe, this time to change, this time to shout in liberated proclamation, it is you who makes us free!

Lord, we pray for the church. We see the body of Christ tormented by sin and sensationalism, torn by heresy and neglect. Teach us never to love these, but to love the church, to defend what is holy and yours. May we regale you with adornments of proper worship and our constant faith.

We pray for the infirmed and the dying. Come unto the shores of the suffering and wash them free of their temporal gloom. Gentle sorrowful hearts and cleanse all illness and disease.

Merciful God, we pray for victims of earthquakes and fires. We pray for all lives that remain in harm's way. For places of conflict, we pray for their deliverance. Grieve our hearts to know that in this world we have not been peacemakers. We pray to you to save the souls of those who fall under the terror of our own bombs and weapons. Trim wicked desires that threaten the races. Pluck peace from the flames of war, and make of it an altar where all may worship you.

As we enter this new week, we pray to dignify you by our choices, to be thy good and faithful pleasure. For while Christ will never die again, our preservation belongs to you. Be our seal and our salvation, for we ask this and all our prayers in the name of Jesus Christ. Amen.

### RESOURCES

PRELUDE MUSIC: Variations on "Simple Gifts" (Traditional Shaker Melody)

HYMNS: (from *The United Methodist Hymnal*, 1989)
"God Who Stretched the Spangled Heavens"
"Come, Ye Sinners Poor and Needy"
"Come, Thou Fount of Every Blessing"

SCRIPTURE: Genesis 1:1-5; Psalm 86; Romans 6:1b-11; Matthew 10:26-36

SERMON TITLE: A Whisper, a Shout

SEASON: Fifth Sunday after Pentecost; Ordinary Time; Summer

EVENTS: Earthquakes, forest fires, priest sexual abuses, U.S. "war on terrorism"

# STONES REMOVED

DORA M. ATLAS

I was born in 1921 in Ramseur, North Carolina, in a family of ten children. A larger group of us children regularly played church down in the woods. We made our musical instruments out of easy-to-find items. Pot lids became cymbals and ale tops were joined together to make tambourines. We had the music and all we needed was a preacher. The Holiness Church in Ramseur, North Carolina, already had women preachers, so it was not unusual for me to think I could be the preacher for our childhood church. I preached on the same theme every time: "Here is the Lamb of God who takes away the sin of the world…" (Jn. 1:29).

Our family moved to the town of Asheboro when I was a teenager. I was made aware of my call, and it was dramatic. In a vision, I saw the face of one whom I recognized as Jeremiah. Immediately, I consulted the book Jeremiah, and to my amazement, I found these words "Before I formed you in the womb I knew you, / and before you were born I consecrated you; / I appointed you a prophet to the nations" (Jer. 1:5). After reading the rest of Jeremiah and about the troubles he encountered, I was not willing to accept the call out of stark fear. The first and the biggest stone in my call to ministry paralyzed me completely. Many years later, after I moved to Hempstead, New York, when I became very comfortable and more knowledgeable with the scriptures, I recognized that the stone had been removed and I had not even noticed. I was engrossed in teaching Sunday school and Bible study in my church where I was an active member. One particular Sunday school lesson was from Luke 13:34, which tells of Jesus' brooding and grieving over Jerusalem like a mother hen. It was a wake-up message, and I was overwhelmed by the stone of guilt, and felt I was about to be destroyed. I repented and yielded myself to the call on my life. I shared with Albert, my husband, and the rest of my family that I desired to go to seminary. I chose Hood Theological Seminary in Salisbury, North Carolina. My local church set a time for a trial sermon with plans to recommend me for ministerial standing. The reverend at my local church had said I "had the gifts," but he did not recommend me to the Conference for ministerial standing. Nothing happened for a year until the next minister encouraged me to go to Hood.

I accepted the call at age fifty-two, after forty years of ignoring the call. By then, I had been married for twenty-three years and was the mother of three offspring and two foster children. My husband Albert was the sole breadwinner. Stone number three was getting prepared to preach.

I was a full-time housewife and mother with no income of my own. My husband, who was reared in the Southern Baptist tradition believing that women should not adorn the pulpit, was definitely not giving any money to support my becoming a preacher. Before we were married, we discussed our religious differences and we agreed not to interfere in each other's faith practices. Now he expressed his sentiment that he did not expect this being a preacher to go this far. Neither did I. I had grown up in the Methodist denomination and did not share the belief that men only could be preachers. My husband and I had gone to our separate churches and were both very active members. I was Superintendent of Sunday School at Jackson Memorial AME Zion Church in Hempstead, New York. My daily study of the scriptures for classes and Bible study was considered by him to be all the preparation needed for my call to ministry.

I found it heartbreaking to give up my foster children who had been with me about three years. I needed to get a job and save money enough to pay my seminary expenses. God moved the stone of closed doors before I recognized some of them. Landing a job at my age with no experience was a breeze after I prayed about it. I expected my husband to come across with board money since I was bringing Paul, our nine-year-old son, to Salisbury to live with me. No, he felt I should pay all my expenses. Our eldest and only daughter, Jean, was in her third year at college in Durham, North Carolina. Our middle child, a son, Edwin, was in high school and would stay home with his dad. When I felt I had enough money for travel, tuition, and books, I sent my application to Hood Seminary in Salisbury. The seminary dean received my application and promptly let me know he had no place for a woman student minister and her young son. I prayed to God about this stone of rejection. During the same summer, another dean, who sent a letter to welcome my son and me to the campus at Hood, replaced that dean. When I arrived on campus and while I was registering, Dean Walter Yates informed me that a scholarship was waiting for me. This freed up funds for boarding expenses—another stone (of deprivation) removed by Almighty God. Additionally, I was offered and accepted the offer to work as on-campus dorm matron for a stipend. I strongly believed that God blessed me through all these hurdles, rather than punished me for waiting so long to heed the call. At one point, I was down to my last meal—a hamburger for my son and cereal for me. The next morning, an unexpected check from a dear friend arrived in the mail. God had done it again! God moved the stone of hunger. Then God softened the heart of my husband, who started sending money routinely.

In March 1972, I preached my initial sermon, which was required by the denomination before one became a candidate for licensing. The different forms of ministry that I have had the opportunity to do range from being an associate pastor in spiritual counseling to founder and director of Our Daily Bread, a soup kitchen for the hungry. I was associate pastor at Jackson Memorial AME Zion Church in Hempstead, New York, about two years. For another three years, I was assistant pastor at Marable Memorial AME Zion Church in Kannapolis, North Carolina, where I did the spiritual counseling. I was assistant pastor at Wesley Chapel AME Zion Church in Asheboro, North Carolina, for approximately one year. I was most discouraged and disappointed that I was not appointed to a position as pastor in the AME Zion Church after receiving a bachelor of theology degree at the Zion Church seminary. There were some males appointed pastors who had not even been to seminary. When I was selected by the First Congregational United Church of Christ to be their first female pastor, I felt God moved another stone and loved me more than I loved God's institutional church. I accepted the UCC's offer because it gave me a greater sense of worth and confirmed my belief that God had a special place for me to serve as pastor. I liked the UCC polity for its autonomy and inclusiveness, and joined the denomination. Being in the United Church of Christ afforded me more freedom to follow the guidance of the Holy Spirit. I found the congregation to be welcoming and most accepting of me. The congregation made available to me all the UCC resources (including the acronyms). The Association and Conference persons were as receptive. One active member always accompanied me to the various meetings. I am a native of Asheboro and was impressed that I was offered a pastor's position in my own hometown. I served that church for nine years before retiring. For a retirement gift, the church gave me a trip to the Holy Land.

The spark that prompted my retirement was a revelation I got at a Pilgrimage Retreat at Blowing Rock that was sponsored by the UCC Southern Conference. The retreat offered self-examination through worship, praise, and silent meditation for twenty-four hours. My nonchalant attitude about serving in the four walls of parish ministry was pierced by a stark realization that my ministry could go beyond the set parameters of the institutional church.

I became involved in several peace and social justice programs. I served as a charter member to organize a local prison chaplaincy program after the North Carolina Prison System dissolved the state-supported chaplaincy program. Locally, the hospice agency, a fledgling one, offered training classes for volunteers and I attended. I served as a volunteer, giving hands-on advice, making home visits, and being a chaplain when needed. I worked on the board of Battered Women's Shelter. I agreed to be on call for spiritual counseling. I even housed some of the women at my home. I was also involved with Habitat for Humanity.

In my youth, I remember being concerned about the hungry in my community. Our family carried meals to other people often. Biscuits with sugar and butter were one of the items we really enjoyed giving to others. Later in my life, I began to hear God speaking to me further about feeding the hungry. Led by passages of scriptures, I became aware of the hunger surrounding me.

After visiting in Hempstead, New York, and while awaiting my return train at Penn Station, I observed homeless people raiding the garbage cans. All the way home, I knew I had to do something about the hungry in my backyard. My plans were to fund the hunger program with my Social Security check. My expectations were to feed about a half dozen persons as an extended family. To my amazement, twenty-one persons showed up on opening day. The news media reported that Our Daily Bread ran out of bread. The public responded immediately with food, finances, volunteers, utensils, paper goods, and so on. The first year of operation, we fed over ten thousand meals. The program still operates with total volunteer giving—the food, cooks, office workers, servers, the funds, and other sundry services after twelve years. This is a faith ministry and everyone who believes that Jesus wants us to feed his sheep has a role to play in this ministry. The kitchen operates five days a week and offers a hot, well-balanced meal without cost to its patrons. All patrons are welcomed regardless of age, race, religion, or other differences.

At first, it was difficult to find a suitable place to begin. In the meantime, a day care center was relocating and I was able to lease the building from the Asheboro Housing Authority (AHA) for $1 a year. After nine years, AHA began reneging on the mutual agreement. The stone of discouragement loomed when they suggested that we seek housing elsewhere, and I felt we would be forced to close the kitchen.

Little did I know that God had already designed the new place just across the street on a vacant lot. I talked with sympathizers who networked and decided that a special building could serve as a home for the soup kitchen for many years to come and would be free of other agencies' interferences. A capital funds committee was organized with volunteers, and they pooled their ideas and made the community aware of the dilemma. They campaigned for cash, pledges, and commitments, and within six months, $150,000 for a specially designed building of 2,068 square feet was raised. The community had responded overwhelmingly. The building was constructed by Mark Trollinger, an architect and builder. We moved in the week of July 4, 1999. At the dedication ceremony, the board of directors named it the Dora Atlas Building. All food is donated and no charges are made for the meals. Everyone who is hungry and cannot afford to buy food is welcomed at this table of Our Daily Bread.

I am still a member of First Congregational United Church of Christ where I preach occasionally. I have been blessed with opportunities to preach in both black and white congregations since retirement. I miss the opportunity to expound on scriptures, but I am certain that I am where God wants me to be presently.

# A CIRCUITOUS ROUTE

KAYE W. CRAWFORD

When Pearl Harbor was bombed, I was a six-month-old infant cradled in my mother's lap when she heard the news. That gigantic moment in American history set the stage for my yet-uncharted life.

Growing up in the small town of Hillsborough, North Carolina, I was nurtured by loving parents, grandparents, aunts, uncles, and cousins. Our family lived within walking distance of the school, library, church, movie theater, and all the local hangouts.

The environment was a safe haven for youngsters to mill about and explore without fear. Just the right space for a creative introvert to observe town happenings and personalities.

When I was nine years old, my leisure time was spent reading biographies, going to Western movies, listening to daily reports of the war overseas, going to church, and preaching on the creek bank behind my home. My favorite biography was about Abe Lincoln (not Mary Todd Lincoln), my favorite Western hero was Roy Rogers (not Dale Evans), my favorite war hero was Douglas MacArthur (not Clara Barton), my favorite preacher was Billy Graham (I knew no female preacher models).

Looking back on my life, I can easily see how I was drawn early to the roles usually always held by males. Sitting on the porch knitting sweaters for the war effort did not pique my interest. Leading troops into battle did. Listening to a women's circle meeting discuss whose recipe was the best at the last church supper did nothing to my increase my zest for life. Preaching to thousands a message of salvation made my heart tingle.

As I preached to an imaginary congregation by the creek bank, I would rant and rail to the wooden cotton-mill bobbins I had set up as my congregants. They could not move. They were held captive by a pigtailed little girl with dimpled cheeks ... a little girl with a message in her heart she wanted to share with the world. I wanted to tell people about Jesus.

My parents saw to it that I was in Sunday school and church every Sunday at the local Methodist church. I often sat with my grandparents whose warm and fragrant bodies did much to add to my comfort level and to my feeling of acceptance. The Methodist church did so much to encourage me as a youngster. I was often called on to pray in group settings. "Now that little girl can really pray a sweet prayer" was a familiar comment. As I progressed through youth fellowship, I was given leadership roles on the local and area levels and represented our church at state meetings. Fertilizer was being added to the seeds of evangelism sown by Billy Graham, but I began to realize that women just did not get to do what Billy Graham was doing.

Then came college and my rebellion. Near the end of high school, I had witnessed enough adult church members misbehaving that I began to lose faith in the church body. College was the setting I needed to find my own identity and a faith for myself. I went to church very little for the next ten years. After college, I worked as a schoolteacher in Virginia Beach, Virginia, for a year before marrying and living in Indiana for three years while my husband served in the Air Force. Upon his discharge in 1967, we moved back to Virginia Beach where I again taught school until our first child was born the following year. Virginia Beach was a hotbed of fundamentalism in that era. Jim and Tammy

Faye Bakker and Pat Robertson were just beginning their ministries in the Tidewater area. I was invited to a charismatic church to a Bible study as I began to have deep spiritual hunger. We then joined the Virginia Beach Methodist Church where we helped start a couples' Sunday school class. The class gained members in eighteen months. The spiritual nature of the class brought nurture to many. Four of us from that class eventually became ordained ministers.

In 1970, we decided to move back home to Hillsborough to get my husband out of the rat race of corporate life and to raise our child in small-town life. It was a good decision.

Our second child was born in 1972, and I stayed home with the children until 1975 when I resumed my teaching career. For the next seven years as a teacher of American literature and journalism, I began to think deeply about spiritual lessons in the stories I taught. At the same time, I became heavily involved in my husband's home church. Becoming a Baptist was hard for me because I had grown up hearing stories about "fighting" and "hard-evangelizing" Baptists. But once I committed to the local church, I jumped in with abandon.

I taught a couples' Sunday school class that became a flagship for drawing members into the church. Among many other roles I filled, the role I was given to develop a day-care ministry at the church was the most spiritually rewarding.

I knew nothing about administration, day-care licensing, or early childhood development. Even though I was very reluctant, the pastor thought I had the skills to do this task and he strongly encouraged me to take up the gauntlet. The day care was a success after the first year and operated for more than twenty years.

After the day-care venture, I became restless in my teaching career and began to feel burned out. My husband, the ever-strong anchor in my life, told me to take some time off to see where God was leading me. I resigned from teaching in 1982. As soon as the personnel committee of my church heard this, they asked me to apply for a part-time job as minister of education. The pastor again encouraged me to consider filling this role. I began my ministry in 1982 and began taking a few seminary courses in the fall to help me learn more about religious education.

The only night classes available to me were in preaching and church communications. I was in the preaching class only a few weeks before I knew I had found my place. I was feeling a strong calling to help hurting people, and I felt God calling me to become a pastor. I entered the master of divinity program at Southeastern Baptist Theological Seminary as a full-time student in 1983. I was forty-two years old. My children were twelve and fifteen, entering the most expensive years of their lives.

My husband Joe and I prayed long and hard about my entering seminary and not working full time. Every time we added up our expenses on paper, the income fell far short. But we were both convinced that seminary was where I was supposed to be, and we figured God would take care of the rest. A few weeks after I had made this decision and had told my church about it, I walked in to my church office and found a check for full tuition for the first year on my desk. A group of five women from the church, several of whom were only nominally involved, had taken on my going to seminary as a project of passion. If I had ever doubted my call to seminary, the doubt was totally erased that day. From that point on, I never looked back or wondered if I had done the right thing.

In 1984, halfway though my seminary training, I sought ordination from my local church. In most Baptist churches, no training is required for ordination ... just a "call." The Hillsborough Baptist Church was one of the few in the state that would ordain women even as deacons. The church unanimously supported my call to ministry and ordained me shortly thereafter.

By the time I finished seminary in 1986, the pastor had recommended my position be changed to associate pastor and my hours increased to full time. The North Carolina State Baptist Convention named me to be the founding pastor of a mission church in Hillsborough and this became a joint position as I continued to serve as the associate in the mother church.

At the same time, the crisis in the Southern Baptist Convention (SBC) was deepening the divide between fundamentalists and moderates. The chief complaint of the fundamentalists was that seminaries were corrupting students with "liberal teachings" by using the method of historical-critical study rather than an inerrancy approach to Bible teaching.

In 1987, the pastor I had worked with for seven years accepted a call to another church. A Southeastern seminary professor was called as interim pastor. The SBC crisis was at a boiling point. Both the interim pastor and I tried to help our congregation understand the dangers we saw in the developing storm. We told them of a ten-year-plan to take control of all major SBC institutions. Eight of those years had already passed. Our information caused some to bristle and go on the defensive. Some realized they believed what the fundamentalist leadership believed and that the interim pastor and I should stop the diatribe.

In 1988, the pastor search committee called a minister to preach a trial sermon. Some of the church members did some research on their own and found the candidate to have fundamentalist leanings. The war was on. The candidate was voted down, the church was badly divided, and I was the messenger who needed to be killed. A vote by the membership showed more votes against me than I would have liked but not enough to oust me. I stayed on another year and found the climate becoming increasingly hostile. Some members shunned me; others treated me with outright disdain. The pain for my family and me was immense. My husband and my children were becoming increasingly uncomfortable in their home church. During that year, I began to talk to the United Church of Christ about possibilities for my serving as a UCC pastor. The denomination had made a national resolution years before in support of women as pastors. They helped me through the "privilege of call" process, and I began interviewing with a church in Virginia. I also was still a student at Southeastern working on a doctor of ministry degree, which I received in 1988.

At the same time, the local Baptist church called another senior pastor who was not a fundamentalist but who had an authoritarian leadership style. After his second week on the job, he told me I would no longer be assisting in the pulpit but would keep the nursery instead. He did not want me to make pastoral calls or hospital visits unless he was unavailable. I could tell he probably had been given direction by someone to bring me under control. The handwriting was on the wall. The next day I resigned. Immediately, my phone began to ring with questions of "why don't you start a new church in Hillsborough?" My response was, "I'm going to become part of a different denomination." They said, "We will too." I said, "You don't know anything about the United Church of Christ." They said, "We'll learn." I told them I was exhausted from all the rigmarole and I would be taking thirty days off, not wanting to talk to anyone. They took it on themselves to invite Conference and Association leaders from the United Church of Christ to teach them about the denomination.

At the end of thirty days, a group of about thirty people had formed and was making plans to begin worshiping together. The Southern Conference of the United Church of Christ had offered them an unoccupied church building in Mebane to use rent-free until they could decide what they wanted to do. The group asked me to preach for the month of July in 1989 in what became the Hillsborough Congregation. By November, the church was received into the United Church of Christ and I was officially installed as pastor. On that day, the church had fifty-one charter members.

Within thirty months from the day the church first assembled, the congregation purchased land and did much of the hands-on construction on the first building. The building was occupied in November of 1991. The church has been very involved in offering compassion to the needy in the community and the world. The members have helped build four Habitat for Humanity houses, raised over $10,000 for AIDS patients, fully supported five to ten families in Bangladesh every year for ten years through sales in the church's Third World gift shop, provided school supplies for needy children in the community, participated in twelve CROP Walk events, led worship at the prison, sent seven students to Germany on relationship-building tours, sent one member to Guatemala on a Habitat trip, and supported numerous other local and worldwide missions ... all this by one hundred members. In addition, in 2000, the church made the decision to become an Open and Affirming church to gay, lesbian, bisexual, and transgendered people. That decision was probably the most rewarding time in my twenty years of ministry. Only a people filled with deep compassion and with a strong commitment to following the way of Christ would do that. Serving as their pastor has been an absolute joy.

When I was installed as a UCC minister in 1989, I did not realize I was the only woman in the state serving alone in a full-time position as senior pastor. Several women were serving as part-time pastors and one was serving as a copastor. In the fourteen years since, those numbers have increased and will probably increase radically in the next generation.

Now, as I enter retirement years, I reflect on my pilgrimage and marvel at the changes in church and in my own beliefs that have occurred in the past fifty years. All my beliefs no longer coincide with those of Billy Graham. Women have taken on more leadership roles in the church. I no longer feel alone as a female pastor.

I have been extremely blessed to have a husband who has been tenacious in his support of my ministry. Joe kept my car serviced, the house clean, and money in our pockets when we needed it. Our two children, Kristin and Chip, have lived their lives with integrity and have always been supportive of my unusual role. My parents grew in acceptance and understanding of my call to ministry and were fully supportive all the way. Numerous friends throughout the years have reached out in very kind ways to show their love for my family and me. Having a supportive family and friends can make the load so much easier.

I came into ministry late, but the journey has filled my life with meaning and purpose. I am grateful to have been on the cutting edge with other women who felt the call to serve as pastor and have been given that privilege. The journey has not been easy, but this road-less-taken has been a life of adventure filled with immeasurable spiritual rewards. I hope the road will be more open and accessible to women yet to enter into this holy service we call pastoral ministry.

# FAREWELL TO HUCC

March 7, 2004

▩

KAYE W. CRAWFORD

As pastor of Hillsborough United Church of Christ since its beginning in 1989, I have received many blessings. The greatest gift I have received is the gift of grace that has been given me when I have made mistakes, have disappointed people, or when I have failed to be as sensitive as I should have been.

Another wonderful blessing I have received from the church family is a willingness to become a congregation filled with diversity. Throughout the years, we have received members with roots in twenty-five different denominations, people from pagan experiences, and people with no faith in anything.

In the beginning, I had a vision that we would become an interracial church. I thought we would have members from the African American community, but that has not happened. We have had a number of speakers and choirs from that community, and we have occasionally worshiped with them. While we have not had African American persons join our membership, members of our congregation have adopted children from Chile, Russia, Korea, Guatemala, and one is expected soon from China. It is so wonderful to see these families crossing cultural and social boundaries to welcome these children.

We also have adult members who are natives of France, Germany, and Palestine. Our pianist is a fourteen-year-old Jewish young man, Gene Plesser-Goldstein, who had never played a Christian hymn until he came to work with us more than a year ago. His musical talent is extraordinary, but his loving spirit is even greater. His presence and manner have helped our congregation deepen our understanding of and respect for our Judeo-Christian heritage. His young sister sometimes plays the violin for us. Their two mothers have been a blessing to us as well as they have shared the wonderful family they have created together.

In 1999, Olu Menjay, an African intern from Liberia who was a student at Duke Divinity School, brought with him a deep sense of what it means to be committed to God in the midst of strife. He found our church to be a nurturing place as he prepared to return as a minister in his conflicted homeland.

A gay intern served with us several years ago because she particularly desired a congregation that was Open and Affirming and that had a woman pastor. She was a blessing to me and to our congregation as she ministered among us with her warm and loving spirit.

On weekdays, our church campus offers space to other groups. We have people working in our buildings daily who are from backgrounds that include Portuguese Catholic, Hispanic Catholic, Hindu, and Buddhist. We have had a good working relationship, and we have learned from one another.

Other ministries that occur in HUCC space are Narcotics Anonymous, Therapeutic Foster Parents (a support group for adults who are providing a temporary home for children in need of intervention), KidSCope/ Childscope: preschoolers with behavioral difficulties, and a Social Anxiety Disorder group.

Our Open and Affirming congregation has become a spiritual home for a number of gay, lesbian, and bisexual persons. Sexual orientation is not a barrier for full participation in the life of our congregation. This congregation has been gracious enough to use inclusive language in our materials, in most of our music, and in our liturgy. Inclusive language does so much to give an equal place to all. In addition, hearing God spoken of with female imagery does much to broaden the scope of our spiritual understanding.

I do not cry today because my journey here is over. Instead, I smile because I was able to take the journey at all. I am a woman most blessed.

# AT MAMA'S TABLE

Annual Meeting of the Southern Conference UCC, Elon University
June 14, 2001

▦

KAYE W. CRAWFORD

SCRIPTURE: Luke 24:13-35 (The Road to Emmaus)

*This sermon is a re-creation of a message delivered without a manuscript for morning devotions at the Southern Conference UCC Annual Meeting on Friday, June 15, 2001. The situation in our Eastern North Carolina Association that is alluded to involves the rejection of a new church start in North Raleigh, North Carolina, that was denied admission into the Association in October of 2000 because it was an "Open and Affirming" (the designation used in the United Church of Christ when a local church decides to welcome and fully include in its life and ministry gay, lesbian, bisexual, and transgender people) congregation.*

After the crucifixion, two of Jesus' disciples were on the road to Emmaus, pondering what had happened, trying to make sense of it all. Where had their leader gone? How could such an awful thing have happened? Some of the disciples said they had seen him, but where was he now? Their leader had been taken from them. Little did they know that the stranger walking and talking with them along the road was the resurrected Christ. Only later, when he was sitting at table with them and breaking bread with them, did they look back and realize it was Jesus who had been walking with them on the road to Emmaus. Then they said, "Did not our hearts burn within us as we walked along the way?"

My mother died this past Monday. I delivered her eulogy on Wednesday. I have had little time to prepare a message for today, but I think Mama's life gave me a message appropriate for our Conference and Associations today and for us as individual persons. Our theme for this annual Conference is "Healing and Renewal." Later in this worship service, you will have an opportunity to come for an anointing with holy oil as the sign of the cross is marked on your forehead. If you have a need for personal healing or for corporate healing for us as churches and Associations that make up the Southern Conference, you may come.

Now, as for my mother and how I think her life sends a message to us today.... Mama learned eighteen months ago that she had an incurable, inoperable tumor. She took the news in her usual stoic manner and quickly announced she wanted to stay at home, and she said she wanted to avoid harsh treatments that might give her more days but little quality. My brother and I assured her we would see she had the care she needed, and we would be there for her.

Six months later, Mom was placed in hospice care but still lived alone at home and remained reasonably independent. She lived for a year after she was placed in hospice care, six months longer than her doctor expected. My brother and I arranged increased care for her as the months went by, but in the last six months he and I were there, offering twenty-four-hour care on the weekends, and we were staying many nights during the week. We had more time to talk with each other than we had in forty years prior. We got to know each other again. We gained a new appreciation for each other. And, as I look back on it, I know Jesus was with us on our own road to Emmaus, loving us, guiding us, comforting us.

After the first six months of hospice care, Mom said to me one day, "I don't know why I'm lingering so long." Considering how advanced the cancer was when first diagnosed, I was wondering the same thing. Now that I have been able to step back a little, I can see how God was at work in all those extra months.

Mama often had comments to make about the importance of family staying together. She was concerned that after she was gone my brother and I might not come together as family. She knew how different we were and that we had had little social contact over the years except for times at her table. Mama was lingering to help us "get our family act together." Mama wanted us to continue to come to the table after she was gone.

My brother and I share the same blood and come from the same gene pool. Beyond those biological similarities, we have little in common. My brother is a Methodist. I am UCC. He is conservative. I am liberal. He has spent his career as a banker helping people save money. I have spent my career as a minister trying to convince people to give money away. Was it going to be possible for us to establish any kind of meaningful relationship? How were we going to do this? These questions prompted me to think about how Mama had kept us connected over the years.

While my brother and I had little contact socially in our adult years, we always came together at Christmas time for a meal at Mama's table. Interaction at the table was sometimes strained, but we tried to stay away from issues we knew would spark a destructive fire among us. We just tried to get along for this one evening, catch up on significant events in one another's lives, tell a few jokes, recall some fond family memories, and exchange some generic gifts since we didn't know each other well enough to give gifts that showed sensitivity to one another's likes and dislikes.

As the grandchildren grew up, they began to ask to bring dates to Mama's table at Christmas. Mama always readily accepted the requests and set an extra plate for the new visitor. About fifteen years ago, the first date appeared at the table. Following a dispute with his parents while he was still in high school, the young man had left home and was living with a friend and dating my daughter. Not exactly the scenario my mother would have chosen for her granddaughter's date, but Mom welcomed him at the table and treated him as she treated the rest of us. The next year, a granddaughter brought an Asian guest to the table. Now that was a first for our family. The year was about 1988, and Mama didn't have any Asian friends. But the young Asian man was given an equal place at the table. He was welcomed. Later, a granddaughter married an atheist … a first in our family. While Mama was disturbed by this development, she did not turn the new in-law away from the table. (The atheist, by the way, acts more Christian than many Christians I see in church every Sunday!) Then a few years later, one of the grandchildren brought a Hispanic date to the Christmas dinner. He was Catholic. Mama welcomed him and made him feel included with the family activities. She really enjoyed his company, and Mama developed a loving relationship with him. Then a grandchild brought a gay friend, who also happened to be African American, to the table. Mama had a wrinkled brow on this one, but she didn't ask questions. She just set another place and welcomed him to the table.

Now Mother had seen many changes in our culture in her eighty-four years, but the fifteen years must have caused her to stretch more socially in her views than she ever had. She had to open her heart to people she never expected to have at her table. She talked some about these new developments over the years … mostly, in a reasoning-out kind of way. In this process, she always remained open to new people from diverse backgrounds … just respecting them for who they were without asking them to show credentials before coming to her table. She had a heart to welcome them all even if she did not agree with their personal lifestyles, or if she was unaccustomed to their culture or social habits, or if she did not understand their viewpoints, religious experiences, or political leanings. All were welcomed at Mama's table.

As Mama lingered on in those last hard months of her life, she referred often to how she wanted us to stay together as family. As my brother and I spent those long nights together giving her care, we had time to hear each other's hearts. We were totally committed to staying with Mom through the hard times, but we were learning to have new respect for each other as we recalled our family stories and memories. We didn't know it at the time, but Mama was giving us time to develop a renewed relationship that would keep us meeting at the family table after Mama was gone.

I've thought a lot about our family story and how that relates to what is going on in the life of our Conference and in our Associations. We have always known that, as a Conference, we are made up of churches with differing beliefs and theological understandings. We have different beliefs concerning some very important issues: the death penalty, abortion, interpretation of the Scriptures, women as pastors, homosexuality, inclusive language . . . the list goes on. We will never agree on many of those issues. To try to force agreement on these issues will destroy us. We hope we can agree on the larger concepts that bind us. Can we agree to love unconditionally, to come together annually to worship and support missions together, to listen to one another, to make room for one another at Christ's table without judgment or condemnation? If we cannot, our Associations and our Conference will be in shambles and Christ's message to the world will be tarnished by our failure to give one another an equal place at Christ's table.

All were welcomed at my mama's table. In the days ahead, we as Conference and Associations will have decisions to make about who is welcome at Christ's table. As we linger through long meetings and hear different opinions, may we find a way to be together at Christ's table. As we consider in our various church settings who will be welcomed at the table, may our "hearts burn within us" as we welcome the risen Christ who is walking with us. May our spirits be warmed by the loving presence of our Savior.

# COPASTOR

## JILL R. EDENS

Two are better than one, because they have a good reward
for their toil. For if they fall, one will lift up the other; but woe to one
who is alone and falls and does not have another to help. Again, if two
lie together, they keep warm; but how can one keep warm alone?
And though one might prevail against another, two will withstand one.
A threefold cord is not quickly broken.

ECCLESIASTES 4:9–12

I am, undeniably, a baby boomer. My parents were married when my
father returned home from the navy after World War II where he
served as a "Seabee" in the South Pacific. I was born, Jill Ruth
Milidonis, in 1952, the second of my parents' three daughters.

My father returned to Fenn College under the G.I. Bill, studied to
become a mechanical engineer, and, simultaneously, set about to start
a die-cast business. White Industries supported our family until his

retirement at the age of 55. My father had a strong work ethic typical of a first-generation American.

I worked at White Industries summers and holidays during high school and college. I was given a chance to do every job for which I had even a shred of ability. I inspected and counted aluminum and zinc castings in the 100-degree heat of the foundry. We worked eight-hour shifts in long-sleeved work shirts, gloves, long pants, and heavy shoes to protect against the metal flash of the castings. Relief arrived when my father promoted me to the air-conditioned office when the office manager went on vacation. Learning how to navigate a small business and how to live in the man's world of die casting would turn out to be a most useful background for leadership in the parish.

We started out as a typical 1950s household in Parma, Ohio, a western suburb of Cleveland. The "typical" part would soon come to an end. My mother stayed at home until we were all in school and then, in what seemed a radical move at the time, she went back to school so she could go to work as an elementary school teacher. Having a mother who worked was a source of embarrassment in those days—my father made a good living after all—but she persisted despite our protests.

My mother was (and is) a beautiful, bright, and adored only child. She skipped the second grade and was assigned to major work, an accelerated program for gifted children in the Cleveland public school system. She was admitted to Bennington College in Vermont at the age of sixteen on scholarship. A bright but very young woman from Cleveland's near West Side, she found herself far from home and living among some of the richest, most privileged young women in the nation. It didn't last. She did well academically but was too far from home. After one year, she transferred to Western Reserve University School of Nursing. Mother was special to her parents from the day of her birth and to my father from the day he fell in love with her. Everyone felt that way about her, including me.

Mom resumed her education at Kent State University at the time of the Kent riots when four students were shot and killed by the Ohio National Guard. My mother's experiences both as a student and as a teacher made a strong impression on me both because of the time and place in which we lived and her persistent commitment and courage.

After completing her work at Kent, my mother taught in the Cleveland public schools for twenty-two years. This era followed the Hough riots and included court-ordered Cleveland school desegregation. Our mother was relocated from the West Side school in which she had taught for years to a predominantly African American school on the East Side. These were difficult and violent times in Cleveland. Mother's school was located in the middle of public housing and poorly secured. One evening she walked to her car to find that her tires had been slashed. She waited alone outside the locked school building for my father to make the forty-five minute drive from the West Side to retrieve her. Later she would be held up at gunpoint while teaching class; the thief escaped with the contents of her purse. She was given a leave of absence to recover from that experience, yet that did not diminish her determination to continue teaching. She was reassigned to an integrated school near the Cleveland Hopkins Airport, where she taught until her retirement.

I so admired my mother that I was determined to become a teacher just like her. I attended Wittenberg University in Springfield, Ohio, and graduated, certified to teach, in 1973. This was the time of the great teacher glut. Teaching jobs were hard to come by and, in the mysterious way in which God works, I landed at the doors of the church. At the age of twenty-one, I was offered and accepted a position as director of Christian education at a United Church of Christ in Hamden, Connecticut, more out of a need to get out on my own and pay the bills than out of a sense of calling.

I had grown up in a loving and active Evangelical United Brethren (EUB) Church. My family actively supported this ministry, and I loved going. My favorite memories include Camp Wanake, a week-long, overnight EUB summer camp that formed my vision of what the Christian community could be. This was an experience for which I longed twelve months of the year and around which I kept up voluminous correspondence with fellow campers. And yet I landed on the steps of the church in Connecticut unable to affirm any faith, certain only of my doubts to the point that I told the search committee that I was uncertain of my Christian faith but confident of my ability to lead educational programs. My commitment was halfhearted at best. I told the committee that I would stay only until I could secure a teaching position. They hired me!

How to explain my loss of faith? Being a product of the 1960s and its penchant for questioning and doubt led me to read the works of skeptics and doubters and to wander from the Christian community. The seed that was planted in the well-tended garden of my early life was neglected. My memory of this time was of the exhilaration of the college experience. Yet, now I can see that I was also grieving my loving home. It is only in retrospect that I now make the connection between this normal experience of loss around leaving home, which I identified at the time as a loss of faith. Certainly, the godlike care and protection of my parents was coming to an end. It was in fact the death of my childish gods; I had to grow up. I became impressed with the emptiness of doubt. Yet, I did not have a way to engage and transform doubt into a faith that could provide a foundation for living. I had loved God my whole life, and I was afraid that I was faced with a life without God. I was honestly searching for a way that led beyond doubt to faith. It was then that I began to serve the church.

The church I served in Hamden was in many respects no different from many UCC churches. It had its share of bickering and infighting. It was a fragile time; the church was seeking a new pastor in the midst of an interim period. Yet, the faith of church people began to make an impression on me. Week after week, they struggled to work out their faith, individually and in community. Even in the most trying times, many of them persisted in Christian faith and church life, and they encouraged me. By the end of the semester, a church member, who was also a faculty member at Yale Divinity School, encouraged me to apply to the master of divinity program at Yale. It never occurred to me to consider the ministry. I had never known a woman minister. I didn't believe that women would ever be accepted as pastors, not to mention that I was still struggling with my own faith. Being a lay worker was easier. I could minister to and be supported by the Christian community in a nonthreatening role that didn't require the affirmation that is ordination. For the remainder of the year and through the summer, I continued to struggle and finally enrolled at Yale Divinity School (YDS). Not that I was more confident in my faith! I entered divinity school with a "prove-it-to-me" attitude. Fortunately for me, YDS had enrolled plenty of students like me, and, through its excellent teaching, chapel services, student body, and my continued work in the church, I found life and faith. I not only met "Jesus again for the first time" but also met the church again for the first time.

One of the many blessings of those years at YDS was meeting another student, Richard Edens. We were married on graduation weekend and in 1978 proposed to be both a married couple and a clergy couple. I had known few women in ministry and all of them faculty or chaplains at Yale. I had never known a clergy couple and had little idea of how that model for ministry might work. Rick had grown up in a Methodist Church in Charlotte, North Carolina. I grew up in Parma Evangelical United Brethren Church. Since the merger, we were both United Methodist. In our last semester, Rick and I met Bishop Jesse Dewitt of the Wisconsin Conference of the United Methodist Church who had come to Yale Divinity School to encourage United Methodists to consider the Wisconsin Conference. We accepted his invitation and I was ordained into the United Methodist Church at Green Lake, Wisconsin, in June of 1978. Rick and I were appointed to a large suburban parish west of Milwaukee as co-associate pastors.

The year in Wisconsin made Rick homesick for his beloved North Carolina and both of us homesick for the UCC, where we had spent all of our training. We leapt without looking into a pastorate where we initially shared one salary in a small parish bordering the campus of the University of North Carolina at Chapel Hill. Sharing one $13,000 per year package of compensation in 1979, we about starved while looking out at a maximum of eighty parishioners on Sunday morning with no more than a half dozen children in the Sunday school. The entire church budget was approximately $43,000, and no parsonage was provided in housing-strapped Chapel Hill. With our school loan repayment schedule kicking in, we knew this could not last. The Research Triangle was a fast-paced and expensive place to live; fortunately, Chapel Hill was growing and United Church along with it. Things were changing.

We have served United Church of Chapel Hill for twenty-five years, from 1979 to the present. These have been the best years of our lives, though by no means the easiest. United Church hardly ever saw a challenge it didn't like, whether calling a clergy couple when no one had any earthly idea about how that might function or opening its fellowship hall to homeless people in order to encourage the town of Chapel Hill to create a homeless shelter. The church sponsored vigorous exchanges with citizens from the former Soviet Union during the height of the Reagan cold war, among many other projects.

Our daughter, Ruth, was born to us in 1983 and all of us wondered how a clergy couple would figure out clergy parenting. (For better or for worse, that will be Ruth's chapter to write!) The opportunity to copastor and coparent is a gift that we will always treasure. United Church was supportive of our goal to share our position so that our daughter would not have to be enrolled in full-day day care. Too often congregations are cited for what they do wrong. It is important to tell the story of what a congregation does right. We were shaped as pastors and parents by our relationship with United Church. The congregation often handled us like wise parents. They never compared us. (If they did, we didn't know about it!) They were indulgent grandparents, aunts, uncles, mentors, and friends to our daughter. They were long on encouragement and sparing on criticism and advice. While these early years were exhausting for us as young parents and young pastors, we look back on them with pleasure and with gratitude to the congregation that helped to make a rewarding family life possible.

In 1986, as the mother of a preschooler and copastor of a growing church, I enrolled in the doctor of ministry program at Lancaster Theological Seminary. It was lunacy, but those were the days of "superwoman." Admitting that I had reached my limits was simply out of the question. I was part of a project supported by the Southern Conference that would develop an alternative track to ordination for pastors already serving in the Southern Conference who did not have a master of divinity degree. The group that originally participated in the project was composed of four African American ministers and one white female minister, me. Because the burden of finding an alternative route to ordination falls disproportionately on African American ministers, the initial summer of the project included the study of the history of the African American church in the United States. I was entranced.

My newfound fascination with the African American church would have to wait. The demands of parenting and pastoring a growing church were growing in intensity. I completed the first year of work and then took an extended leave of absence. I would finally return to the project in 1993. I completed the doctor of ministry program and my dissertation, which described the practice of worship in UCC African American churches in North Carolina, graduating from Lancaster in 1996.

The intervening years were crucial to United Church and to the shaping of our ministry. Starting with the writing of a mission statement in 1989, United Church had grown to the point where expanding its facilities could no longer be avoided. Also, in the early 1990s, the church began the process of becoming an Open and Affirming parish of the United Church of Christ. It was a challenging and rewarding two-year process that ended with an overwhelmingly positive vote of the congregation to become Open and Affirming. This decision accelerated the growth of the parish.

By 1996, conflict in the parish over how and where to expand had reached a crisis. The writing of the dissertation for the doctorate became a welcome retreat from the unrelenting conflict. Chapel Hill loves its historic village-like atmosphere, and United Church loved its historic downtown building no less. Relocation seemed unthinkable, even to the pastors. Several years and considerable expense ended in the sad knowledge that United Church could not accomplish its goals in ministry in the confined precincts of the downtown site. The plan to renovate our beloved church facility had to be abandoned. More years of small group meetings, endless process and conflict, which made the Open and Affirming decision seem painless by comparison, finally ended when in 1997 the church purchased land for its new location north of town on Airport Road. Hope began to infect all of us with the hiring of an architect who would help us create a new site for ministry and mission. Of all the challenges Rick and I have engaged with each other and with our church, none was more difficult or rewarding than relocation. It caused us as a congregation to name our identity and commit to our ministry. We worshiped for the first time in our new facility on Easter Day in the year 2000.

The heart of my calling is evangelical. I have tried over these past twenty-five years to bring people to life and faith in Jesus Christ through his radical message of inclusion. I believe that he calls all people in every time and place to follow his word and way regardless of race, gender, ability, or sexual orientation.

United Church has grown from 80 in worship to 450 in worship through its inclusive and expansive ministry. It has welcomed Iglesia Unida de Cristo, a Spanish language new-church-start that nests with it. More recently, United Church has welcomed the Ismaili Muslim Community to worship at United Church three nights a week. Together with Iglesia Unida de Cristo, the Ismaili community and the Judea Reform Congregation, United Church has completed an inter-faith—Christian, Jewish, Muslim—Habitat House in the past year.

I have been richly blessed to serve with my husband Richard and with this gracious and bold congregation that has been so steadfast both in conflict and rejoicing. My heart is full of gratitude for this rich and complex ministry.

SERMON

# ONLY LOVE GUARANTEES FREEDOM

**United Church of Chapel Hill, October 27, 2002**

JILL R. EDENS

SCRIPTURES: Deuteronomy 34:1–12; Matthew 22:34–46

I hardly attend a church event these days without someone, knowing that I am of Greek ancestry, asking if I have seen *My Big Fat Greek Wedding.* The answer is yes. I went to see it twice. I did not grow up in that kind of Greek household because my mother is not Greek—but the volume levels were about the same. I grew up in a home in which everyone felt perfectly free to express themselves, usually at the top of their lungs. Just to give you an idea of the decibel levels, and Rick will vouch for me here, I am considered to be the quiet, serious member of the family. One year at the beach, my cousin took me aside and gently tried to share his concern that I was getting to be too much of a loner.

I look forward to our big family gatherings; they are great fun. However, Rick, who comes from a well-behaved Southern family, was shell-shocked after his first Christmas with my family. He remarked, "Even the little five-year-old walks around waving her hands and expressing herself at full volume." There is hardly a topic about which our family is neutral. Everyone feels deeply about something and doesn't hesitate to share it.

When we are with my family, no one wrings her or his hands worrying about what somebody might say. We do not spend much time mulling over these interactions once they are over. Why? Because we love one another and enjoy one another. That kind of love has been the bedrock of my life. It is what makes me free. I am glad that my country makes me free, but really, it's love that guarantees my freedom. It is love that created the community of freedom into which I was born. It is love that sets us free to think and say what we believe is true, to cry, but mostly to laugh together, to embrace and to know that no matter what, my family will always be there for me.

Some of us take that freedom-creating love for granted, but for others, the raised voice is a horror and a searing threat to well-being. For some in this free country, there is no freedom. There is only the defenseless self, desperately seeking protection from random attacks on its vitality. For some it is a life where abandonment is ever near, always lurking around the next corner. Freedom and joy have no content where love is not also faithful and kind. Only love guarantees freedom.

We are all grateful this week that the sniper's reign of terror in the Washington area is over. Mona Charen wrote Friday in *The Chapel Hill Herald* about what should have been a routine visit to her local Costco. She writes, "The place is so popular that it's usually difficult to find a parking space even in the midst of a downpour. But last week, on a pleasant fall afternoon, Costco was sparsely populated. Making your way across the parking lot, the hair on the back of your neck stands up. Even if you know, as everyone does, that the chances of any particular individual being shot by the sniper are minute, you cannot help thinking about it." She concludes, "The sniper may or may not be a terrorist . . . nonetheless he was robbing Americans . . . of their security and their peace of mind."

The description of the Costco parking lot is familiar to me. I grew up in the Cleveland area during the Hough riots and the desegregation of the Cleveland public schools. Fear emptied many parking lots in those days. And, there weren't just two snipers, there were lots of them and not all of them African American either. My hometown, Parma, Ohio, was armed to the teeth. And I can tell you, nothing is more terrifying than a bunch of frightened white people with guns.

I remember wishing that my parents would protect us by buying a gun. So my sisters and I asked them why we didn't have a gun as our neighbors did. This didn't seem unreasonable to us because our mother had been held up at gunpoint in her kindergarten classroom on the East Side of Cleveland. My parents calmly responded to our accusation that they were security deficient by pointing out that if we had a gun someone would probably take it from us and shoot us with it. In those dangerous times, our family habits never changed.

This insistence on not changing family habits regardless of the violence or threat of violence also meant that we were required to learn how to navigate public transportation. My parents let me ride the public buses by myself everywhere, even to the Cleveland Art Museum to take a class when I was in high school. If you know where the Cleveland Museum is, even the most liberal-minded among you might wonder at this decision. Yet, part of being an adult in my house meant learning how to navigate public transportation, my parents were as adamant about that as they were about not having guns. And so, I went to Wittenberg University as a freshman from the bus station in downtown Cleveland, through Columbus, and on to Springfield, Ohio. A memorable trip, let me tell you. I was always firmly planted right behind the bus driver. I have had many years to think about this and to feel grateful that my parents did build a sense of security in me by choosing, quite intentionally, to set me free rather than to keep me safe.

They came to Jesus and asked him, "'Teacher, which commandment in the law is the greatest?' He said to him, 'You shall love the Lord your God with all your heart, and with all your soul, and with all your mind.' This is the greatest and first commandment. And a second is like it: 'You shall love your neighbor as yourself.' On these two commandments hang all the law and the prophets." Without the love of God and neighbor, the law that protects human dignity, guarantees human freedom, and regulates human interaction, has no place to hang. It has no mooring; it literally falls down.

Jesus' second commandment to love your neighbor as yourself comes from the book of Leviticus and comes from a larger passage that says, "You shall not take vengeance or bear a grudge against any of your people, but you shall love your neighbor as yourself: I am the LORD" (Lev. 19:18). The purpose of this commandment in Leviticus is Moses' instruction to the people about how they shall live in a new situation of freedom in the promised land. This new country calls for new ways of living. Only love of neighbor will guarantee freedom in the land of promise.

Paul says it too, "Love does no wrong to a neighbor; therefore, love is the fulfilling of the law" (Rom. 13:10). Paul, more than any other Christian preacher, understands that only love interrupts the chain reaction of evil; only love can transform enemies into neighbors; only love will sacrifice itself for the other. Paul warns about the downward spiral of evil when those who are impatient in hard times only invite increasing impatience and added suffering. Those who refuse hospitality to the stranger are in turn refused hospitality. When cursing prompts more cursing, the chain of recriminations continues unbroken. To laugh at the misfortunes of others guarantees mounting hostility. When evil is repaid by evil, when every injustice is met by the demand for vengeance, harm grows in geometric proportions, poisoning everything it touches.

We are sometimes tempted to think that love is the icing on the cake. Love is a luxury that we can afford once we have taken care of our security—usually by stockpiling our wealth and strengthening our defenses. Yet, Christian faith insists that love is not a luxury made possible by protection afforded by our wealth and our weapons. Love is a core requirement for life. To follow in the way of love is to release the age-old human desire for security. To live in love is to accept that the way of love requires us to live both with risk and with unfinished business. Every offense is not going to be met with retribution if we follow Jesus' way. Only love breaks the cycle of evil; only love protects human dignity; only love guarantees freedom.

To live in this way is counterintuitive. Instead of strengthening defenses, we make ourselves vulnerable. Instead of the comfort of closure, we live with the awkwardness of unfinished business. We do not first seek to clean up the messiness of life or to level the unevenness of experience. First, we live with it and seek with patient hearts to understand. We don't need to explain at first why life unfolds the way it does, but instead, learn to welcome its twists and turns. We come to understand that life lived in love and freedom is untidy and not guaranteed to keep us safe. It is full of unfinished business and future uncertainties. The way of love shows us how to live creatively and faithfully with forgiveness and to refuse to seal life in the tomb.

The wisdom of these scriptures offers this subtle teaching about how to live with freedom: to live self-consciously and lovingly and faithfully toward a future that we do not control but that we can, with God's help, shape and transform. The most important tool in our toolbox for this job is forgiveness. Only forgiveness can keep love alive, keep us free, and keep life open to the future.

Christopher Lasche's book, *The True and Only Heaven,* says that the "grand narrative" of our nation, the great "story line" of our society, is our faith in progress. Progress is the grand story we tell about ourselves. It tells us that we have a definite past with which we can be done and finished, and it promises a predictable future that we can control. Neat endings and predictable futures are not life—not this life anyway. Will Willimon once said, "Life is an accumulation of decisions that could have been made differently, baggage called regret, faces we will never see again, words that came out wrong, and things that don't go as planned." In a place governed by love, time is not wasted second-guessing the mess. Accumulated regret and obsessive second-guessing are paralyzing. In the place that chooses life and is governed by love of neighbor, forgiveness and acceptance free the community for faithful action.

Where there is love there is freedom and there is a future for life because God's purposes for you and for your world are not utterly dependent on your getting it right. You can go ahead and live, not knowing how it will turn out and not having to make it turn out. It is not up to you and to me to fix everything before we can do anything.

My favorite part of *My Big Fat Greek Wedding* is where the mother tells the daughter to take the risk of going to school—to live her life. This is why this mother gave this child life. It is also why God gave us this life—to live it, in faith and love and freedom. Amen.

# A STORY OF ANGELS

MARY EMMA EVANS
*(As told to Robin J. Townsley Arcus)*

I started in ministry a long, long time ago. I always felt I was a special child, but I didn't know why. I was always very friendly; people always loved me, which I thought was because I wasn't the prettiest child in the family. *Pretty* in the African American family is fair skinned and long hair. And if you happened to be the little black child with short hair, which was me, you have to do something to get attention, you almost had to disobey. I learned I had something very different about me, in my special reaching out for others. I was very compassionate toward people, especially poor people, picked-on people, people whom I felt were different from myself. I always felt I could do something to make a person better. In school, I would look for the left-behind kids and try to befriend them, but, of course, that meant that since they were picked on, then I would be picked on too.

The bullies in my day were powerful, and people were afraid of them, which meant they got more undeserved power. I think it's the same way now. Whenever you stand up and speak the truth to power, you get beat up.

As a little girl of eight and nine years old, the thing I remember most is loving church more than anything in the world. I just loved church. I would think about attending all the time; during the day in school, I would be hoping I could go to church on Sunday.

My mother had so much responsibility on her. My dad left home when I was two years old—I'm the ninth child—so my mother didn't go to church much. My brothers and sisters didn't seem to love church the way I did. But each week I would be planning and wondering if I had something to wear. In the black church, you always have to be well dressed; you don't just attend church in your everyday clothes. My mom would say, "If you can find something to wear to church, then you may go."

There was a lady down the road by the name of Beulah Fisher—I guess that's why I still like to sing the song "Beulah Land." My mother said, "If you go down to Ms. Fisher's house and walk with her kids to Antioch Christian Church, I'll let you go."

There's an amazing part to this story I've been reluctant to talk about because when I tell it, people have mixed reactions. Some start looking at me as if there's something wrong with me.

We lived on a farm, and we were about a mile back in the woods, which when you walked seemed like about two or three miles. I would start out from the house to get to the highway, to Ms. Beulah's house. The minute I would get to where the heavy trees filled in on each side, I would start running, and something would pick me up and carry me. I would not come down until I got to the highway. It sounds crazy, but it's the truth. I was lifted, like being carried. And the minute I would get to the highway, I would be placed down, like Mary Poppins. This would happen to me every Sunday. It got to where I would look forward to it.

I guess I was about twenty years older before I told anyone about being lifted, and they said, "Are you sure you're all right in the head?" It took telling this to someone who believed in angels for me to be believed.

Now I remember one particular time when I was walking out to the road from the farm. It was a white folks' farm, and my family were sharecroppers, which meant that someone else owned the land and we would work on their farm. At the end of the year when the crops were all sold, the black folks got half the money, maybe.

One day, when I was about ten, I was walking along the road when the man who owned the farm stopped and asked if I wanted a ride. Everybody thought well of him, so I said, "Sure." I felt good thinking that I was riding with *The Man*. Before long he turned down this side road, and I just thought, *Well, he's checking on his crops or something.* He turned to me and asked if I had ever had sex. I said, "No." I just trusted this man so much. He was sitting on the seat there at his side of the truck; I was sitting at the other side. He was looking at me all strange. Then all of a sudden he started fighting with something at the window that I couldn't see, and he was saying, "Get away! Get away!" I was wondering what was happening because I was looking around and didn't see anything. In no time, he started the truck up and pulled out real fast; he was looking back and asking me if I could see it. I said, "See what?" He said, "Didn't you see all those things at the window trying to get in the truck?" I think they were angels from down in the woods who were chasing him. He never did touch me.

So the man took me on to Ms. Beulah's house, but he never did bother me again. It took a long time for me to realize that he was planning to rape me. I was so innocent minded. But I know now that's what was going to happen. So the Lord protected me in that area. I believe that right then the Lord was preparing me for ministry by allowing me to witness his power.

I attended Antioch Christian Church until we moved and I joined Oak Level United Church of Christ. I was baptized at Oak Level. I remember being particularly concerned about funerals. I couldn't understand that I would hear gossip about people, but when their funeral would happen, suddenly only nice things were said. And so I would ask questions. I couldn't understand what happened once a person died to make them be so loved. Of course, in my day, the older people at the church would say, "You're talking too much," or "You're asking too many questions," or "Just you shut up, Girl." They thought you were being sassy when you asked strong questions. I have that problem today. We have some pastors and preachers now who feel like you're not as important as they are, so when I ask those strong questions, speaking truth to power, I witness a lot of this resistance. I think I'm still the little girl inside a big girl, still with the same spirit, asking some of the same questions.

One of the things I dislike with a passion is hypocrisy. I think people ought to be able to be real. As a girl, I would sit in church and wonder about preachers who would preach about how Jesus would feed people, how Jesus loved the hungry and the homeless. Then those same preachers would lift the offering, but they wouldn't help anyone with that money. They knew people who were poor; they knew my mother was very poor, and so I often wondered why they didn't take some of that money and help my mom. I remember asking some of those questions but I would get the same response: "You're talking too much."

My struggle was why people couldn't just go on and love other people. I never could get any answers.

Another thing that would upset me, and maybe this was the way the Lord was preparing me for the type of ministry I'm in, I used to hear preachers preaching against smoking cigarettes, but the same preacher would rush out to the tobacco field on Monday to go work in it. I said, "If it's a sin to smoke it, isn't it a sin to grow it?" Well, I became Lucy's (my mother's) big-mouth little girl because I wanted to know. Today I don't understand why people reject Open and Affirming, pull out of the United Church of Christ, but support gay musicians in the church.

Different things would puzzle me, like why people would say one thing and then live another. I used to wonder why we used to take a lot of dinner to church. There would be all this chocolate cake, fried chicken, and potato salad, but they didn't want the real hungry people to eat it. They wanted to save it for the big-shot people. I used to see all this, and when I did, I would say to myself, *When I grow up, I'm going to change this. I'm going to "feed the hungry."*

I grew up, went to school, and at sixteen, I got married. I dropped out of school, started having babies, went back to school, and received my GED [general equivalency diploma]. People in the church took for granted that I had a lot of education, which must have been how I presented myself, because at that time, I didn't. Educated people would seek me out, encourage me, and motivate me. I never understood why.

I got out of my ugly state, and grew up tall, slim, and pretty. Even after people started telling me I was pretty, I didn't believe them. Now that I'm older and not so pretty I'm more apt to believe them! (Smile)

When I got married, I started working in my husband's denomination—the United Holy Church of America. I worked in that church for nearly eighteen years. I ran into the same problems in that church. At the opening of the church service, they would sing a spiritual song, but I would say, "Why don't we sing a hymn, something to prepare ourselves for worship?" But the people said, "You're just being a goodie two-shoes." I was saying, "Let's not start with something that's just been laid up last week, that hardly has any substance." But they would not accept me for who I was. They would preach against wearing lipstick, against wearing slacks, against going to the movies. If they would see a man talking to a woman who wasn't his wife, they would think he/she was running around. The Sunday school lesson would start out with Moses and they would end up turning it into someone's adulterous lifestyle. There was this list of things you don't do.

The pastor was a very strong man. He was not an educated man, but highly intelligent. I was called to preach there in 1981. I preached my initial sermon in that church, but in 1982, I left—I had to leave. I just couldn't stay in that denomination. When I left, they predicted I wouldn't make it, but what happened was that I really excelled in ministry.

In 1983, I was called as the first African American woman to pastor a UCC church in the Eastern North Carolina Association. I have never been honored for it, though. I began pastoring Union Grove Church. My home church pastor at Oak Level is the one who encouraged me to come back to the denomination. He made promises and offered his support. I am sure he was instrumental in my becoming pastor at Union Grove Church. And so I just started moving into any area of the United Church of Christ that I could and learning everything there was to learn.

I started taking classes at Shaw Divinity School in Raleigh. That took four or five years. I would go on Tuesday nights with about twelve or fourteen other pastors from various churches around Henderson, North Carolina. Then I entered another course at Shaw that involved going to school on Saturdays. That continued for about another two years.

Then, I started at Lancaster Seminary in Pennsylvania in a course of study called Pastor's School. I would go up for two weeks every fall. I did that for about another nine years. It seemed like I was always at Lancaster. I completed that course through the support of the Southern Conference. The Conference encouraged pastors to get our education in other ways because some of us didn't go the traditional route of four years of college and three years of full-time seminary.

But even after Lancaster I wasn't through yet. I enrolled at the American Theological Seminary, where I took classes in Henderson and Millegeville, Georgia. It was another three years when I finally received a master's degree in practical theology, but the United Church of Christ doesn't acknowledge the degree or recognize the school.

I will say that whatever courses the United Church of Christ offered, I took.

I had a pleasant start at my first church, Union Grove United Church of Christ here in Henderson. My trouble began when a man came to join the church as an associate deacon. He was a very likeable young person, so much so, he more or less became the star of the show. That was all right. He and I had become good friends. But the women of the church who adored him thought he was giving me too much of his attention and not giving enough to them. They used to talk. I didn't like how that was going. I was experiencing flashbacks of why I had left the previous denomination.

About that time, I had a very good friend encourage me to leave that church, a friend who was also a UCC minister. He was one of the ones who would travel to Lancaster. We called ourselves Godbrother and Godsister. Now he knew nothing about this young man in my church. But one day my friend said, "You have outgrown Union Grove. They are taking advantage of you," which was true. They weren't paying me but one hundred dollars a month. To me that didn't matter because I was so excited about being a pastor. I was also working for the telephone company so I was making my own money and wasn't suffering for anything. He would call me on the phone and say, "I think you need to resign Union Grove." So finally, it got into my brain that maybe I did need to leave.

One night, when we were having a business meeting, I looked around for something to write on, and grabbed a small paper sack. On that paper bag, I wrote my resignation and told them I would give them a more formal resignation later. So I left that church. Two months later, this man who was my friend, the one who encouraged me to resign, became pastor of that church. And he brought along with him a woman to be his assistant pastor. (However, I don't think she was aware of the deception.) She is still the pastor of that church today. That was some of the deception I witnessed. And he was a *Four-and-Three* [four years of college and three years of seminary]. He knew I didn't have some of the education that the other pastors had. But I was thinking, *Why would he go to a church that pays only one hundred dollars a month and he's got a college degree and seminary training?* Well, I think it was to get another pastor there. When she started as the pastor, they immediately began giving her what they had been giving him, which was eight hundred dollars a month. So they went from discriminating against me to giving him eight hundred dollars a month, and it wasn't because of his seminary training, because I was filling the church. They liked my preaching and plenty of people were coming. But the church started paying him eight hundred dollars a month and when he left, he encouraged them to continue giving her what they had been giving to him. It was really a gender thing—men in the United Church of Christ have much power.

After this, I went back to my home church, but I was never able to hang around my home church because people were calling me to preach in other churches. I would get sometimes two and three calls for a single Sunday. I was called by a pastor in Chapel Hill who said he just had to have me at his church. So I consented to go to New Covenant United Church of Christ in Chapel Hill. They had a very good pastor there. But he would sometimes need to be gone on business on Sundays. So when he was gone, I would fill in, and when he would return, the people would brag about my preaching style, so much that he became jealous. I got a letter from him one week that said I had led a song before I preached the sermon, and he didn't think I should have done that. So every time he would leave and come back I would get a letter that he wasn't satisfied with something I had done. I told my husband that I had to leave that church because a lot of jealousy had set in. It was a gender thing.

Then, one day I was riding in my telephone truck through a poor, drug-infested neighborhood in Henderson, where I saw a man raking leaves near a church. I said to myself, "That is the church; I'm going to be their pastor." Then I thought to myself, *Why do you want to be over here?* But I stopped the truck and went over and asked the man if they had a pastor. He said, "No, ma'am. We have no money here. We can't get anyone to pastor our church." And I said, "I would love to be your pastor." And he said, "You would?!" He said, "You're the girl in the telephone truck and you want to be our pastor?" And I said, "Yes, I would!"

He said for me to call his sister who was the overseer of the church. So I called her up and she said for me to go ahead and pastor. So I had my first service there two Sundays later, and we had 178 people in that church. Later that afternoon we had 75 for a second service. From then on, we didn't have enough parking space or seating space in that little church. So I pastored West End Holy Church. The thing is, they never have had a man pastor, only women ministers, and that church had been there for ninety years! I worked faithfully there for approximately six years—on second Sundays members from Oak Level would help fill the church. The pastor quickly began second Sunday services at Oak Level which had neer been done before.

Then I was called to Alston Chapel United Church of Christ in Sanford, which is where I am today.

In between time, there were a lot of overtures from one of the UCC ministers—I mean romantic overtures, not professional ones. But I never took this man seriously because he'd done a lot of joking with me. I remember one time we were in Pittsburgh, Pennsylvania, for General Synod, and he said, "Mary, come walk with me up to my room." People were open with each other since it was Synod, everybody being friendly to one another. And I was just so honored to walk with my friend. So we went in this big hotel up to his room. When we got there, he said, "I want to say one thing to you and I'll never say anything else as long as I live—I just want to kiss you." I said, "Why?" He said, "I promise it won't go any further than that." So I said, "All right." And when he started to, right then the telephone started ringing, just like when they say *saved by the bell*. It was someone from our group wondering where we had parked the car, so we had to go down and deal with that. Once we started downstairs, I thought to myself, *This man actually kissed me, and this is another pastor!* I started feeling so guilty. I thought people would think we did something, and then I thought, but we *did do* something! I was all sweaty feeling and guilty. And yet, he acted as though nothing had happened. I'm sure he thought nothing really did happen. For many pastors, something to women means nothing to them.

I was so glad for that telephone, and I was thinking that it was like the way I was protected by angels when I was young. But this time I was a grown, married lady. I'm sure I should have said no. But then I thought about how I was in his hotel room and how that must have seemed. It made me think about how people say, "What was that woman doing in a motel room if she didn't think something was going to happen to her?" When something like this happens to you, you think differently about other folks' situation.

So after that I couldn't be friends with any other male pastors without this man getting upset. One day he said to me, "Mary, what is your greatest fear?" And I said, "Failure." After that he said, "I could help you if you will let me." After that conversation I feel he set out like Saul after David to destroy my influence. I said, "What is it you think I need to do?"

He said, "Well, Mary, you are a very pretty woman. You know all those men are looking at you. And you know those men's wives are looking at you. It will be another fifteen or twenty years before you pastor another church." He had called me to his office to tell me this. And there I went, just so happy to be called to my minister-friend's office. He went on, "You know those women don't want you around their husbands." I was sitting there feeling like, rather than treating me like a pastor, he's treating me like some kind of woman with another calling other than ministry.

He kept saying, "I could help you." The last thing he said to me was, "Mary, you are like a tornado. You know when a tornado or a storm is in the air, and you start preparing, getting water and canned food? And then the storm just skips right over you, and you're sitting there all prepared for nothing." He said, "You're not as naive as you pretend you are. You're always smiling. Mary, you know I want you!" And then he said, "If you are good to me, I'll help you move up." At that point I did not feel like being "good." Many pastors today will accept women in ministry if they are "good." I thought to myself, *Are all these men whom you look up to, do they just want you for a piece of meat, or a piece of property . . . for you to obey them?*

If you are an African American woman preacher, it helps for you to be young, pretty, and friendly, and to be able to preach well. You need to be able to present yourself as controllable by men, especially the ones you are working under. You need to be available. Availability carries with it a certain amount of joy and a certain amount of pain—it depends on what they want you to be available for. It carries with it something most women fail to discuss. We don't discuss it in women's conferences; we don't discuss it sister to sister. Most of us protect our men's shortcomings, and we do not talk about the pains that have been inflicted on women in the church by male pastors. A lot of women tolerate in men the things they expose in women.

Most women are ashamed to admit, certainly African American women, that we move up in ministry as far as the men in the church allow. Most of us, when we get to what we consider the top, we don't want to look back and say that we moved up because we allowed the men to control us. I have moved much more quickly in the United Church of Christ even than many of the highly educated women preachers. But, there was always a feeling of *expectation* deeply rooted in the men who helped me to excel. And when this *expectation* was not fulfilled, many of them tried to assassinate my work among the churches. This is something you don't hear from women because if they tell it, they become cancer to the body [of Christ]. So it's been much more painful than I have allowed people to see. But I do need to say, it has not been from all the men, just the ones who, as the Bible says, have rule over you in many cases. There are more "good" male leaders than bad.

My husband knows about the things I have gone through. He is not a very talkative person, but he has allowed me to be a pastor. And when I have wanted to talk about sensitive things, he has not held it against me. So I think one of the ways I have been able to survive sexual harassment in the church is that I have a strong husband who I could go home to and cry, and he would not take off for the church and attack the man or attack me. Thank God for my husband's support.

This is a real problem among African American churches. I'm not sure it isn't a problem in the white churches. I do know that in the white churches that if the preacher marries more than once, the church doesn't seem to hold it against him. In our churches, if you marry more than once, you're considered an outsider. But they will allow the men to do whatever they want inside the marriage. And the women will protect the men, but they won't protect one another.

I don't mean to present my life as a sob story, but being a woman in ministry is not a pretty story. I think the women clergy don't really want people to know, because they live in fear of people treating them differently. Again, it's speaking truth to power, and the men of the United Church of Christ are the power. They will make you or break you. There are more God-sent makers than breakers.

But, I do need to say, a lot of the male ministers have made me, in a positive way—I've had Conference ministers and Association ministers who have been real brothers in the truest sense. In fact, I don't like to travel alone, so one of the older pastors became my mentor, my protector. When I had to fly, he came with me. He became the pastor I needed, my protection away from home. And this man is as pure as the driven snow. He became the father I never had—highly honorable, top of the line. If I could have picked a dad, this is the man I would have picked. So, I don't want to paint a picture that all men are bad, that they all want to jump in bed with you. Some really are genuine. If it had not been for men in ministry, I would not have made it as far as I have. It's just that it only takes a few men—or women—to pull you down. In scripture it says, "If God be for you, who can be against you?"

My dream is for people to love one another. But now we are running into the Open and Affirming issue in the United Church of Christ. This has been going on for four or five years. It started out as a whisper and now it has erupted into a shouting match. The black churches have always welcomed gays and lesbians, but they didn't put a label to it. Most of us have musicians who are 100 percent gay, and we know it. But when it comes to affirming it or speaking it, they say, "No, we'll pull our churches out." It's another thing I don't understand about African American people. Some are very hypocritical.

I stood up at one of the Eastern North Carolina Association meetings and made my speech about including the Open and Affirming churches in our Association. I said I have been discriminated against all my life—I was born poor, black, and female—three strikes against me. And yet, I was called into the ministry, as a woman, then a pastor. I said, "Those of us who sit here who are my age, we know we are a group of African Americans who have been discriminated against one way or another. We know what it's like not to be able to go into a restaurant because of the color of our skin. We don't speak like other people; our educational backgrounds are different." I said to them, "I didn't make gay and lesbian people; therefore, I can't judge them. I've been judged all my life for some reason or another. And I feel that as ministers we should be more sensitive to God's people than the world is. I may not understand what it means to be gay, but I don't need to understand to know how they feel." After I said this, all of a sudden, people I loved and who loved me realized I was on the side of the so-called funny folk. And they went right on, in church even, talking about gays and lesbians in awful ways, in Jesus' name—and put it on the Lord. I thought, *You are asking me to discriminate against another group of people—I cannot do that.*

So here I was again standing up for those who are different, in a great big old Association meeting, saying that we need to love all people, black, white, gay, lesbian. All people should be welcomed to the Table. One of the women from my church was there that day, and it seemed like after I said that, this woman decided to do everything imaginable to get me out of my church. It's just this woman and a group that she's put together, not the church officers. She's been around to the houses of people who haven't been to our church in four or five years, talking me down. She's trying to run me away from *her* church, saying my leadership is no good. But she couldn't get me out. Still, that didn't stop her. She then had another woman take out a warrant against my daughter. My daughter didn't even know this particular woman. This particular woman claimed that my daughter said, "I'm gonna get you." So we had to go to court. We were found not guilty, but that didn't settle it either. We had the

Conference minister come and preach my anniversary service. They called him all sorts of names. It hasn't stopped yet.

From the time I took a stand against those who discriminate against gays and lesbians, everything changed. This lady worked behind me by having letters written. It's this same group that has been instrumental in getting the church to be financially broke. The country people, the good people, have begun staying home. When the good people asked what charge was against me, the only thing they could come up with was my unorthodox way of preaching.

One Sunday, when the chairman of the deacons was making the announcements, this lady walked into the church with three or four others, and passed me a letter. I glanced at it, thinking it must be an announcement. But when I opened it, the letter was telling me I was being dismissed from the church. She then walked over and handed an envelope to the deacon. I thought it must be a copy of the one she had given me.

I said to her, "We will take this up at another time."

By then, he [the chairman of the deacons] had opened and read his letter. He turned to me and said, "Pastor, I believe we need to read this."

I was thinking, *Oh no, maybe they're all in this together.* I must have had a look on my face.

But then he said, "Trust me." So the deacon chairman began to read *his* letter, which turned out to be a letter dismissing *him*. After that, I read my letter of her dismissing *me*.

The chairman said to her, "This is not the procedure. You are out of order." So she just told us we were all wrong, that we were dismissed and to be out of the church directly. She said, "If you're not out, we will padlock the church," and out the door she went.

Meanwhile, we went on with our service. About 12:45 P.M. we saw two police officers come into the vestibule of the church, looking at locks and things. The deacon chair went out to take care of this. The police officer told him someone had called and said that the pastor had been dismissed and that the members had barricaded themselves inside the church. So all of us went outside.

The officer said, "No law has been broken here. This sort of stuff normally doesn't hold up in court. I hope you can resolve it on your own."

When I was first called to be the pastor of that church, I told them that if they ever wanted me to leave, they would need to give me written notice, and that if I needed to leave, I would do the same for them. So I said to the people, "If you want me to leave, I will." But the people said, "No! You're the best part about this church!" So my spirit has told me it is not yet time for me to go. These incidents have not shaken my faith. I still get up each morning looking around for someone else to love.

Other than all that, I've had a very meaningful, rich, productive ministry, in the church, in the community, within the state. I guess I'm one of the most well-known pastors in the area. Even with the pain, there are many more blessings than burdens.

In addition to the church, I am active in many types of ministry. I have an informal program of feeding people. I'm on the state board of my sister's food pantry, but that's really not my calling. I'm just on her board. My ministry is taking my own money, which is very limited I would say, and spending approximately $250 a week feeding people. I have never been the type of person to look into programs and write a grant. I feel like if I had someone to help me in that area, I would have one of the largest ministries in Henderson, or in the county. That would be ministry, just not from a pulpit. A *love* ministry—a church without walls.

The way the Lord is leading me now is to work in city government, to bring unity to city hall, where I think the Lord is going to use me to help unite the city council. What happened was that the city council members wanted me to work on different boards, but every time they posted openings, the incumbents would get the positions. So they started a new "Clean Up Henderson" committee, of which I'm part. They say this is the largest committee the city has ever seen. We mainly clean up junk like abandoned cars, get abandoned structures torn down, clean up all the overgrown and weedy lots; we're carrying away old refrigerators and appliances that people have dumped. We're trying to get industry to move back into Henderson because we don't have a lot of jobs. We have been busy cleaning up Henderson and from doing that I've picked up a lot of other problems—hunger, domestic violence, clothing needs, people needing someone to talk to. This has become a bigger ministry than anything I've ever been in.

From that I decided in 2003 to run for a seat on the Henderson city council. I won by a 60 percent margin—and over a man! I'm really excited about this. The strange thing is I won without any money for a campaign. I didn't set up a committee. I didn't ask for donations. I guess the whole time I ran I had about $250 that people had given me, whereas the man who ran against me had people giving him that much at one time. So I think the Lord is just showing me favor. And from this experience people have begun to call. But it concerns me that some of the issues they call about I can only pass along to other people.

I feel that my ministry is going out into the world, at least the four-county area. That's a big place for me. I don't know how the Lord is going to work it. I want to be discovered, which I guess I have been by Nancy Keppel and Jeanette Stokes with the CD they are producing of my singing, that might bring in money. The first song I recorded was "Peace in the Valley."

So I think the CD, maybe this book, maybe all of this, will bring some money for me to do the things I want to do. My mom kind of crippled me. She said not to ask people for money. But I feel like if I had a way to let people know—hey, I have a vision, maybe you want to get involved—but I really don't know how to do it. But I would love to have some money to clothe children. At least three times a month, maybe more, I'm called on from the schools saying there's a child whose pants are too small, he just split right out of them. Living here, I learned how to get clothes to kids. Sometimes I go to the Salvation Army or to yard sales. I keep clothes hung in my closet. And then, when the need arises, I go take the outfit to the school. That's my ministry.

I'm just about fed up with the four-wall ministry because most people are not serious in what we call the church. We call the church the building, but it's not. So here I am still being the girl on the school grounds who loved the underprivileged people. I was poor myself. I was probably the poorest kid of all, but I didn't know it because I had a lot of love. And for that reason I always thought I had something to give.

As a city council person, I feel as though I'm more a servant than ever. I just can't get myself to feel like I'm a big shot in town. I'd like to feel like that just once, but I don't know how to have those feelings. I'm still trying to feed people and get them shelter.

I've had a radio ministry that has been going a long time. I'm on the radio in Oxford and Henderson. I also do TV ministry, but I use someone else's slot because I cannot afford TV time. I've always funded my own radio program. That's why I don't have much money, because I use most of my money for ministry, especially for sick and shut-in ministry. The radio brings many needs to me—people who need food, visitation, all kind of things.

I guess I'm still looking for angels to pick me up and keep me going. In a way they are. Angels come in so many forms. If I just stop and consider for a moment, I can feel that they are gathered around me, they really are there, and they are carrying me still.

This is my story. This is my song. I dedicate this essay to all who have a story to tell and I hope someday they will meet an angel like Nancy Peeler Keppel who is one of God's "chosen ones" with a definite purpose in life—to reach. So if you miss me from singing and preaching down here, come on up to heaven, I'll be singing and preaching up there.

# THE CALL

SALLYE HARDY

lthough I was born into a Methodist parsonage family, raised in Southern evangelicalism—complete with camp meetings, Sunday night services, altar calls, and conversion experiences—it never crossed my mind that I might be a minister. My parents say that as a child, I would play church with my two older brothers, insisting that they direct the choir and play the piano, while I preached. "Can a four-year-old hear the call?"

In high school, I wrote a paper about how I was going to be an anesthesiologist. My Aunt Katherine had told me I was smart and I ought to go into medicine. My own research showed me that an anesthesiologist did not have to do the bloody part and this assignment demanded that I choose an occupation. Anesthesiology seemed like a good one. So when I entered college, I declared a premed major.

My first premed biology course convinced me that medicine was not going to be my life's work. During my days at Asbury College, I considered being a missionary. The slides we were shown from other countries were beautiful. Travel was appealing, and if you were a missionary, you were definitely doing God's will.

The closest I actually came to foreign mission work was dating a guy from Kenya. By my junior year, the pressure was on to declare a major. All of my friends, it seemed, were well on their way to careers as teachers or doctors or marriage. I had more hours of credit in physical education and psychology than anything else, so I declared a physical education major with a psychology minor and graduated with a teaching degree. What else did women do?

Twice I served as a youth director in large United Methodist churches. Both times, I was successful. The youth came to church, and most stayed with the group. Those were the days when to be Christian meant you might be against a war; you might sing with a guitar in a sanctuary; and you might have long hair and not be a girl. They were the days of the new *Good News Bible* and before the days of Christian ministry degrees and *GROUP* magazine.

I learned that churches could meet real needs in people's lives and be a place of great joy and friendship. Active youth groups create conflicts. Lay staff is vulnerable to the opinions of any church member. My experience as lay staff was that I was easily dispensable. Inevitably, I would upset someone and the senior pastor would always protect himself or herself. Church employment was not safe work for me.

So, I left the life of the church and became an employee of the state at Lynchburg Training School and Hospital. Lynchburg was the largest institution for the mentally retarded in the world, and the world was in the process of deinstitutionalization. It was an exciting, challenging time, but I missed worship. I missed slipping into the sanctuary for times of meditation. I missed being taught and I missed teaching.

After two years, I began to slip into the sanctuary of the local United Methodist church. Eventually I volunteered to work with the children of the church. To salvage a dying children's choir, its devoted director, two other members, and I created an alternative, the Sunshine Kids. It was a club that met on Sunday evenings and combined puppetry, vacation Bible school–type lessons, and *choir*.

The kids came for supper, brought any friend they wanted to, got a T-shirt, and had their own newsletter. It was a fun time, even for the newly energized adults. One Sunday evening, in the midst of children finding their coats, parents finding their children, puppets being "put to bed," sets being dismantled, kids screaming for each other, and adults screaming at the kids not to scream, my pastor, Jim Rush, whispered in my ear, "You ought to be a minister."

That was the first time I ever heard God whisper in my ear. The next morning I went to his office, "Did you say, I ought to be a minister?"

"Yes, I did."

"Why do you think that?"

"Well, don't you love what you're doing here?"

"Yes."

"Don't you like doing this church stuff more than working for the state?"

"Most of the time."

"You teach, you preach, you care about people. You really ought to consider being a minister. Think about it."

Well, I did think about it. I imagined it. I dreamed it. I called my closest friends who knew me, who knew churches. I read and reread scriptures. I diagrammed the pros and cons on yellow legal pads. I went to the sanctuary and pretended it. I researched it.

There were a lot of hoops to jump through. By spring, I had been approved by every committee necessary and been licensed as a local pastor in The United Methodist Church. That fall, I would enter that small Southern seminary with the big basketball team—Duke.

Nurtured in church all my life, I am a spiritual mush. Almost any hymn can bring me to tears. Almost any one's story can bring me to offer a hardy amen. Almost every biblical story makes goose bumps rise on my arms. I have always loved a good preacher, but it was not the powerful sermon, or the stirring song, or the guilt of a spirited altar call that led me into the ministry. It was the soft whisper in my ear of my aging white male pastor, who knew who I was, and brought God's call to me. His casual comment in the middle of children's chaos changed my life, and he was right. I really ought to be a minister.

## Preparation

My whole life had been preparation for ministry, even without my realizing it. As a preacher's kid, I saw daily the blessings and the curses of church life. The same parishioners who brought you fresh vegetables or homemade ice cream often brought gossip with them. Living next door to the church meant that your dad was close when you got off the school bus, but it also meant that you never ate a meal that someone wasn't stopping. The people who thanked God aloud for their pastor and his family may well be the people encouraging the pastor to leave in June. I never quite understood the inconsistency. I still don't.

My southern Christian tradition believed in the individual working of God in people's lives. I had seen the power of God in many ways. I had seen lives transformed by apparent religious experiences. I had seen drunks become sober. I had seen very sick people healed. I had seen those having affairs return to their spouses and be faithful. Church life prepared me to expect something from God and to believe God cared about real life.

As the minister's family, our door was never shut to anyone. My parents would give the shirts off their backs to a stranger and never mention it. They regularly took in "the least of these." They were serious and consistent in their service to Christ. My upbringing prepared me to take the faith life seriously, as a viable choice for my life's work.

When I entered Duke, I was student pastor to four churches, foster mother to one mentally retarded son, an expectant mother of my daughter, and a wife. I had married a charming younger man the year before. While our friendship may have been good, our marriage was not. In my first semester of Duke, we separated. The timing was crucial. I was too far into the semester to quit. I was committed to my preparation to preach.

Despite the dismay of my district superintendent, the people I served and I did well. When the baby came, the people were thrilled. I didn't just survive; I thrived as a pastor, a parent, and a student.

Duke was lifesaving for me. I commuted all four years in a student pastor car pool. In the car, both conversations and coffee were plentiful. Often the times of silence and sleep replenished my body. There were no car phones. The roads between Chatham, Virginia, and

Durham, North Carolina, were sanctuary. My life became a routine of taking care of my church folks three days a week, reading and writing papers, and enjoying every moment with my new baby and foster son.

Education at Duke was revolutionary for me. The distance between what I knew and what I had felt was true began to narrow. For example, I knew the word *he* was used throughout the New Testament and in every sermon I had ever heard preached. The day I discovered that the Greek had neuter endings for many words arbitrarily made masculine by English translators, I was liberated to a new level of existence. It made sense now.

I could handle translators being sexist; I just couldn't handle Jesus being sexist. Inclusive language is still a high priority for me. I insist that God is all genders and no gender—especially to the women and girls entrusted to me.

Professors at Duke were passionate and competent. They were walking proof of people living by what they believed. Father Roland Murphy would recite a psalm as smoothly as saying his name, and suddenly point right at me, and say, "So what has this old psalm got to do with you today?"

In American Christianity, the connection between our country's history and the state of our churches became apparent. The intertwining of our social history and our spiritual institutions encouraged me to believe in the possible relevance of the church.

In Women and Ministry, I had to confront how I could request ordination, in the light of Paul's restriction on women even being teachers of men. I learned not to be afraid of the hard questions, but to embrace them. I became a knowledgeable biblical feminist, not just a woman who wanted to believe she could do anything a man could do.

I explored the differences between ministries and secular services. I developed a theology of creation, of children, of transformation. The Bible and its relevance for today increasingly fascinated me.

It was my preaching professor who taught us to preach the text—preach its content and its form. Dr. Eslinger introduced me to a concept called imaging: putting words together to create an image in the listener's mind that brings them into the text. We might teach a topic, he would say, but we *preach* a text. I set out determined to become a wordsmith. My love for the text and the desire to make it "take" in people's minds still rules my life practices. I remain intrigued by sermon preparation and delivery.

In class after class, conversation after conversation, the walls that divided my life experiences and my beliefs broke down. My experiential foundation was being cemented together by new knowledge. I was being equipped to be a minister.

Before my senior year at Duke, I went out of state to do a ministerial practicum at Lake Junaluska Assembly. When I returned home to Virginia, I was summoned to court for a worthless check for $10.86. I was advised by counsel to plead guilty, and I did, only to find myself facing sentencing in the middle of my last semester of school. Requests to delay the case until after I graduated were denied.

I notified my Duke community through my dean of students, Dr. Paula Gilbert, my class president, and a representative faculty member. Dr. Gilbert made a commitment to do all she could to ensure I get my degree. She vowed she would not let me forget my ministerial calling.

So in my last semester at Duke Divinity School, I spent four out of every seven days in the city jail. On Monday nights, my parents would leave my car parked outside the jail. On Tuesday mornings before dawn, a matron would give me real clothes and a key to my car, and I would leave the jail, drive to my car pool, whose members thought I was coming there from home. On Thursdays, I would return by 6 P.M. to the jail having completed a week's worth of classes, seen my children briefly, and salvaged as much of my life as I could.

No matter where the incarceration, the key is that the incarcerated do not control their own lives. They are always in lockdown to some degree. They make no choices about what they will eat, only if they will. It is not up to those detained to choose who they spend time with, only whether they will fight the time or learn from it. The sounds and the silences inside a jail are magnified by the hardness of the cement walls.

My first night, locked down with only a distant exit sign for a light, a jailer sitting in an office somewhere turned the radio on and through the jail's speakers came, "Kyrie Eleison." Even in my basement cell, in the darkness of a strange place, God found me. The song was popular and often we heard the Latin refrain, saying simply, "Lord, have mercy."

In jail, I met folks guilty of crimes more minor, even more than my own, but serving more time. In jail, I learned how little control we really have, and sometimes it isn't all that bad. In jail, I learned that every person, even the guard and the meanest inmate, has a heart. In jail, I learned that my world could live without me.

While in jail, I experienced the power of women connecting with and for each other. Unlike most incarcerated women, I was sustained, rather than sacrificed. My sister and her roommate took care of my children, opened the day care early, made sure lunches were packed, slept away from their own home, so my children could have consistency and familiar surroundings. My daughter's godmother gave up every weekend to be there. My mother prepared meals, wrote notes, accepted collect phone calls. She even typed papers and mailed them in to my professors, since I had no access to such equipment.

And Paula Gilbert kept her word. More than once, I assisted in student chapel; wearing a suit, wrinkle free because it was pressed between my two-inch mattress and the metal bed frame in my cell. Her confidence in me took her before the Duke faculty to request their approval for my degree, since I had completed all the academic work required.

My final release came on the morning of our baccalaureate, the hooding ceremony for graduate students. Twenty-five hundred of our families and friends gathered in the magnificent Duke chapel. Its towering rock cathedral ceiling and magnificent organ were a long way from the four-by-six-foot block of concrete where I had been the last forty-five days.

"Lift High the Cross" led us to our places. Paula, true to her word, had arranged for me to be a server of communion. Twenty-four hours before, I had been allowed only to wear the issued green jailhouse garb. Tonight I wore my minister's robe, the hood of a divinity graduate, and held close to my chest the broken bread for all.

It was a powerful moment, made possible because of the advocacy of one person, the generosity of many, and God's enormous grace. The day before, the only bread available to me was a piece of white loaf bread, slid through the bars on a lunch tray. Tonight, as I held the bread of life, I knew that call had not gone away.

Duke Divinity School gave me so much more than a great basketball team and a diploma. New knowledge empowered me; the healing of my spirit and my mind decompartmentalized my life; times of solitude tuned me in to an inner part of my soul. Meeting rigid requirements increased my self-confidence. The genuine community, where common needs and goals existed and people were honored for who they were, not who they might become, all created in me a new person, prepared to answer the call on my life.

Although I was well prepared, I was also a single, divorced, formerly incarcerated, convicted felon, mother of two. I was hardly "appointable" by the United Methodists. I would devote my next two years to jumping through the hoops again, proving myself worthy to be ordained a deacon within the United Methodist system. It was a time of great reflection, a reevaluation of who I was, what I believed, where I belonged.

I disagreed with Methodism on many things. I did not believe pastors and churches should be matched based on salary scales. I did not believe the good old boys were really serious about women as pastors. My own bishop told me that churches were not ready then for women, and most women would serve out their pastorates in small, rural isolated places. I did not believe that ministry in a local church was the only place that needed ordained people. I knew I might not be "appointable" for a while and was certainly concerned my ordination would be denied based on that alone. But within the United Methodist system, the needs of local churches always come first.

And I did not believe the United Methodist stated stand on homosexuality. The Book of Discipline was clear that heterosexual marriage was the only place for sexual intimacy. My own experience of sexuality, particularly with how women live and love each other, would not allow their intimacy to be defined as sin. My knowledge of gay and lesbian Christians who lived in faithful, monogamous relationships would not allow me to believe heterosexual marriages to be the only acceptable way for God.

I came to a solid understanding that my life could not be married to such a patriarchal, exclusive, heterosexual system. My divorce from the United Methodist church would be the hardest thing and the best thing I would ever do. It liberated me from a lifetime of trying to please a system that could not be pleased.

In my search for a new church home, I found the United Church of Christ. Oh, my God! It was like a breath of fresh air, a spring of ice-cold water, where meetings were lively and agendas not predetermined by a bishop. People actually made motions and nominations from the floor. I was amazed!

The United Church of Christ leads the religious world in inclusiveness. At its national level, it is openly inclusive of gay and lesbian persons, including their ordination. Our Southern Conference is really integrated. It is rooted in racial and economic justice. At my first UCC gathering, more African Americans were on the stage than white people. A black woman was the president of the Conference, the associate Conference minister, and the keynote preacher for my first General Synod. What a contrast to a stage full of older white males, sitting around the bishop, at every United Methodist Conference I ever attended.

The leadership within the United Church of Christ was elected from the heart of their churches. There was a sense that this denomination was both serious about social justice and rooted in scripture. Almost every UCC minister I met was a transplant from another denomination.

Community United Church of Christ in Raleigh became my spiritual home. Its copastors, Cally and Dave, weekly reminded us that women and men could serve as equal partners in ministry. This church understood that spiritual transformation and social transformation are equal partners in the faith. They beget each other. There was no question that I had found my place.

Where else but in the United Church of Christ could a biblical fundamentalist and a gay pastor sit side by side in a meeting, neither feeling like they had to hide. While both might be uncomfortable with the other, both believed in the other's Christ and that was enough.

During these days, my life's work was with a group of battered women and their children. Again, I experienced the connectedness of women working together. I was the executive director, administering a budget of almost a quarter of a million dollars, coordinating a staff of eight, a board of sixteen. It was amazing to me how much could be done out of a common belief that women should not be battered and children should be safe.

Our staff, underpaid and overworked, connected to each other and to the women we served. Again, I experienced the connectedness in this women's work that was energizing. It made very difficult, dangerous work exciting and fulfilling. Our budget was easily raised, our client base tripled, our volunteers were plentiful. The social transformations in these women's lives were transforming for their spirits.

In the fall, we took a group of battered women and their children to a retreat center called Higher Ground. Protected by the Blue Ridge Mountains and used as our secret getaway, children were free to run and play without fences or deputies. Mothers were free to sip coffee by an open fire and be with each other long into the nights as their children slept.

On our final evening, I asked everyone to bring a rock from the mountain to the fireplace and leave it there. As the sun set, we gathered around the fireplace, which was warm and inviting. The white rocks were piled on the hearth.

The women and children each shared what they had enjoyed most about this time apart . . . the stars, the hayride, being able to run, not having to cook, or just sitting by the fire. I called each person by name, placed a warmed rock in his or her hand, and stated simply, "Don't forget, the God who made this mountain made you."

When the evening was over and the children were in bed (many with rock, under their pillow), and the mountain was quiet under a blanket of stars, I stood in the cold and vowed to my Creator that I would never again give only a stone, instead of the real bread of communion.

In April of 1994, I was ordained by the Eastern North Carolina Association of the Southern Conference of the United Church of Christ to do "other religious work." I was authorized by a church I believed in to do sacramental ministry wherever the spirit provided a place.

## Ministry

There is a constant interaction between my work, who I am now, and who I am becoming. It's like wind and a kite. The kite once in the air, moves and swerves, flies and falls. It allows us to see the wind; we control it through our fingers. That balance of who I am and what I do is often invisible to me. I know that without the Spirit, my kite might fly out of my sight or come crashing down. I also know I control it with the choices I make.

While my work outside the church rather than inside the church has most clearly defined for me my calling and the necessity of my ordination, I have been privileged to serve as pastor over the years.

As a child, I learned the power of story and song and sermon inside the church. They are embedded in my body's cells. I am moved by the very thought of Jesus holding a child in his arms, or being touched by a woman with the issue of blood, or breaking bread and handing it even to the one who would betray him.

I like singing hymns without having to open the book. I have hummed my way through the death of more than one person, watching the music move into their spirit, taking them to their life after death. I study my father's sermons, gather illustrations as if a collector, and prepare sermons even when I have nowhere to preach.

As a pastor, I have had the honor to be invited into people's lives, solely because I was their pastor. I have been entrusted with the secrets of their hearts, the confessions of their souls. I have held their hands when they took their last breath.

As a pastor, I have had the honor of preaching and teaching to an all-volunteer class. I have received people's gifts of time and trust. I have seen the power of ritual, the effectiveness of caring, the need for a safe place for seekers to search.

The people I have served have changed me. It is good work to pastor, if those you pastor want to work. Much of what I love I owe to the church, but the core of what I believe about God, I learned outside of the church.

The mentally retarded I worked with at the Training School taught me the power of presence. Persons without language, without knowledge or reasoning that I can understand, have revealed God to me many times. Our creation is not dependent on what we can think or do, but whom we are when we are with each other. The most profoundly handicapped person responded to the presence of another.

The mentally retarded taught me that the basic need for relationship exists within us all, regardless of our abilities or disabilities. They often jerked me back to simple basic truths. One particular Easter, my foster son John, who has Down's syndrome, was very upset after the Easter service. I could see him processing what he had heard all the way home. He was upset they put nails in Jesus' hands and there was blood. He was upset that Jesus got killed. He knew Jesus loved people, but they killed him. After a long period of silence, he suddenly announced, "Sallye, he got up!"

That is still the best resurrection story I know. John's limited intelligence didn't stop him from understanding the profound theological truth that the grave was empty. The foundation of my own faith was bolstered by John's simple statement. Even today, I am able to believe that not only Jesus but also the rest of us can rise again.

While working with victims of domestic violence who were taking great risks, I learned so much about transformation. There comes a moment, a conversion if you will, when a victim says, "No more," and then does whatever it takes to get out of the violence; they make a new life.

The change begins with a moment of truth, when the sin of violence is acknowledged, not ignored. The courage to name that sin empowers the transformation process to begin. The community who believes the sin should stop empowers the change to continue. That community of support, where basic needs are met, where people share a common vision of nonviolence, where people recognize their need for one another sustains the transformation until it can stand on its own.

Encountering women with broken bones as well as broken spirits taught me the true nature of community and its power. I remember that humanity is the only species with the power to name. Often we are rendered powerless because we do not have the courage to name our own truths. But when we do, our isolation is broken and real change has a chance.

Most of what I know of God, I have learned from children. Every decision I have made since my own daughter was born has taken a child into consideration. From the moment of Jesse's birth, I knew she was not just mine, but belonged to a larger community. Her safety in my womb required the help of friends and medical personnel.

Watching her grow fascinated me. I loved her expressions when you introduced her to a new food. I couldn't believe how her repetitive sounds became words. Her first word was "sock." She could whistle by the age of two. She loved to hear herself do it for hours. I could sit and watch her play for hours. She would squeal with joy over a surprise sock puppet popping up.

Every day I enjoyed her intrinsic nature of joy and play. I came to understand God more fully as a loving parent who delights in her or his children, rather than a father God who disciplines them. Jesse brought genuine joy to my life.

My Jesse taught me the power of trust and time. Her unknowing trust of this inexperienced mom gave us both the time to grow, the possibility of knowing each other. I learned that mothering is not about biology, but about whom we are willing to be.

Jesse's createdness, her genuine goodness from her birth, called into question everything that I had been taught about original sin. Now as a young adult, she continues to confirm for me her divine image. It is expressed through her creativity, her perseverance, her intensity, her determination to discover, to learn, to be self-sufficient, to question. Her times of deep joy and great pain teach me the depth of God's emotions.

My journey through this life has both cost her and gifted her. While she has most often not had financial security or even what she may have needed, she has always known she had her mother's commitment. Sharing life, at its best and its worst, makes it real. Mothering is still teaching me that I am not called to be perfect. I am called to love.

Since 1994, I have owned a licensed child-care center. Again, I have had the enormous blessings and burdens of being intimately responsible for the children of others. In children, I see all those gifts of the Spirit, unconditional love, joy, peace, anticipation, and empathy. I have seen children the first time they noticed their own hands and then realized they could move them.

An infant's body claims for them their power to control what they touch and hold. Within the first few months of a child's life, they learn they can influence another's happiness. But by the time they are two, we have often killed their spontaneity and sacrificed their divine image to our own illusions of what is important.

I have been blessed by children and learned most of what I know of God from them. I have felt God's presence come to me from them as I have rocked them, fed them, and changed their diapers. Their trust is the foundation of faith.

I believe the youngest of children holds the mysteries of the universe. And I, like all of us in ministry, am called to be a steward of those mysteries. It makes sense to me, since children are the closest to the beginning of the creation process that they should be the most connected to the Creator. I can physically feel an exchange of spirit, when I lay my hands in baptism on a baby or lay the bread in a child's hand. I can feel the mystery, as they receive the gift, not encumbered by a past.

I believe Matthew Fox had it right when he articulated the concept of original blessing as the state of our initial creation, rather than original sin. Children require us to be interdependent—mutually giving and receiving respect, care, knowledge, and love. It is no wonder Jesus said, "Truly I tell you, unless you change and become like children, you will never enter the kingdom of heaven" (Mt. 18:3).

My ministries will probably never be traditional, though God knows I have tried to make it so. I know that institutions, religious and otherwise, are preserved by their need to be preserved more than their ability to meet a need. I am increasingly convinced that I am not called to be churched, but to be Christian. I am not ordained to "do" church, but authorized to *do other religious work* by a church that believes that all work is religious. At the time of this writing, I wait. I wonder, *Where will I minister, what will I do?* As I enter this next phase of my lifetime, I seek the gentle breeze of the Spirit to carry me.

# GOD IS GOOD.
# ALL THE TIME.

LYNNE HINTON

I use these words as the title of my life's story because they reveal what my faith and my life as a minister have taught me. This call and response that is often shared in the African American church experience exemplify what my years in the ministry have been about and what I want my life to demonstrate. God is good. All the time.

I was called into the ministry when I was fifteen years old. I was at summer camp and was overwhelmed by the sense that God's hand was on me. Although I had never met a woman minister at the time and was growing up in the home of a Southern Baptist pastor, although the clergyman who spoke to me after I responded to the altar call did not encourage me, it did not occur to me that my call would be denounced or controversial. When I came home, however, and reported with excitement the camp experience and my understanding of it to my father, I soon realized that my call was not normal or acceptable.

It was quite painful to have my father ask me not to tell anyone about this call; I was devastated that he didn't seem pleased or happy. But even at the tender age of fifteen I knew that what had happened to me, that God's hand on my life, was bigger and more persuasive than even my father's disapproval. I knew even in that disappointment that what had happened to me was to be trusted and believed.

Since I had only experienced women in two professional ministerial roles, I thought I had two options. I could be a director of Christian education in a church or I could be a missionary. Annie Armstrong and Lottie Moon, two women missionaries whose names were the titles of the two biggest church offerings of the year in the Southern Baptist Church, were strong influences in my life. Their stories of sacrifice and faith that I heard every Christmas and every Easter made me believe that I would find a place to serve even if it meant I would be sent far away from home. I decided that I was called to be a missionary; and since I felt drawn to work in a health care setting, I set my sights on Wake Forest University to study medicine and become a missionary doctor.

Six weeks into first semester chemistry, my plans and my call were challenged. I realized at the age of eighteen that I was not engineered to take the medical school track. I faltered in college. I felt mostly disappointed, confused. Since I understood my call as a medical missionary, I thought I had failed God. What else could I offer God if I couldn't offer the only thing I thought I could do or be? It was a difficult and trying time for me. I left Wake Forest and attended the University of North Carolina at Greensboro, where I transferred to go into nursing. Finishing that program didn't happen either, so by the time I graduated, I had changed majors too many times to discuss and finally settled in a curriculum that was simply convenient for the classes I had taken.

Although the career in medicine didn't happen, other things did. And even though I realize now that my four years in college were the most difficult years of my life, and even though I felt called into the ministry and yet felt unable to understand that call, honor that call, or feel supported in that call, I was also given some unique opportunities to try out my wings. During my junior year of college, I was hired as the student associate pastor of First Christian Church, Disciples of Christ, in Greensboro. During my time in this position, the pastor resigned, and for a very brief but real time, I served in the pastoral role. A twenty-year-old woman in charge of pastoral responsibilities! God is good! Even in the midst of emotional turmoil, God was making a way.

When I graduated from college, I decided to go to seminary. Since I was still Southern Baptist at the time, I attended Southeastern Theological Seminary in nearby Wake Forest. It was a difficult year in the life of the institution. It was a difficult year for many young seminarians. It was a difficult year for me, and I decided that it was time for me to leave.

Choosing to walk away from the Southern Baptist Church was like choosing to change my last name, choosing to break away from family. For here was the denomination that birthed me in faith, brought me up to believe that God had a plan for me, nurtured me in the ideas that everyone was called to Christian service. But when I began to understand my gifts as gifts for professional ministry, when I began to ask the questions of what else I could do instead of medical missions, when I began to try to speak with my voice to tell my story, I was shunned and silenced and denied. But praise God! Because God is bigger than denominations! God is more creative than church hierarchies! God is good! All the time!

I left the Southern Baptist Church after a year of study at Southeastern Baptist Theological Seminary, and I walked away from everything I knew and headed to Berkeley, California, where I attended Pacific School of Religion (PSR). And here, my life forever changed.

I was introduced to the American Baptists and the United Church of Christ, to many women ministers, to issues of social justice, and the idea that Christianity was more than just "saving souls." I was introduced to the idea that Christianity was about taking up the cross, fighting for the oppressed, feeding the hungry, and empowering the poor. I learned about liberation theology and Bonhoeffer's ideas on cheap grace.

I was immersed in theology and the arts. I took classes in dance and drama. I studied Harlem renaissance literature and Third World American literature. I took Shakespeare and a powerful course from Dr. Katie Cannon that was very influential in my education: Black Women's Literature: Toward a Constructive Ethic.

Everything in my spirit came alive. I was pushed creatively, theologically, and emotionally. Suddenly, I realized that as a woman, as a minister, there were as many opportunities to serve as there were ideas and passionate longings. I learned that there were churches that would call women as pastors, that there were chaplaincy possibilities to work with the dying, with children, with the elderly. I was welcomed into a new world that boldly announced when you say yes to God, God will find a way to use you. And in the midst of all this learning and growing, in the midst of all these possibilities and opportunities, I realized that I wanted to write, that the artist within me was just as real and just as called as the minister.

I graduated and moved back to North Carolina where I married Bob Branard. We settled in a home in rural Guilford County. I wrote my first novel but was unable to sell it so I went back into the ministry track, taking clinical pastoral education and then taking a job working with hospice as a chaplain. I was ordained as an American Baptist minister but was unable to find a local American Baptist church so I attended Mount Hope United Church of Christ.

Just as Pacific School of Religion was a place of great growth and excitement, hospice was also fundamental in shaping who I am as a pastor and as a writer. Here, walking the sacred path of terminal illness, I was taught the most important lessons of life. Every day I spent with a patient, I was reminded of how short and unpredictable life is. Every day that I participated in the death of someone I cared about, I was resolved to be intentional about my living and my loving. Every day I shared with an interdisciplinary team to assist in the dying process for the patient and the family, I was enlightened about the importance of community and working together. I laughed and I cried more deeply than I ever have before or since. I will always be indebted to the holy nature of hospice.

Although I loved my work as chaplain, I still felt unfulfilled professionally and personally. As much as I loved what happened on a day-to-day basis in my ministry, I wanted to preach. I wanted to be in the lives of people not just when they died but also when there was birth and celebrations. I wanted to be more than just a chaplain. I wanted to be a pastor. And with this desire, it seemed God was calling me to the church.

When the pastor of the church I was attending, Mount Hope United Church of Christ, resigned, I applied for the job of supply pastor. I received privilege of call and gained pastoral standing in the Southern Conference. Within a number of months, I resigned from hospice and moved from supply to interim to permanent pastor. This was, of course, not celebrated or honored by the Conference staff. The policy for local churches is that they are not supposed to consider the interim pastor for the permanent position; and I understand all the reasons for this stance. In spite of the unfair advantage that it gives to the interim minister, however, I have found that for many women, it is the only opportunity to receive consideration for the job of senior pastor.

While I was at Mount Hope, I wrote my second novel, *Friendship Cake*. I was experiencing the joy of being in a church community that loved one another, fed one another; and it was from this place of community, this place of feeling as if church was really being church, that I was led to write the story of women in a church becoming friends.

After three and a half years of having served at Mount Hope, I did a pulpit exchange with my friend Rev. Betty Headen, who was serving the First Congregational United Church of Christ in Asheboro, an African American congregation. We simply thought it would be fun, an interesting experience. I did not anticipate what would happen to me. For once again, just as I had felt at the age of fifteen and just as I had felt in becoming the pastor of Mount Hope, I felt God's hand on me. I felt a call to that place. Of course, the circumstances were not in place for me to apply for the position. In fact, it seemed quite inappropriate that I would have such a leaning. After all, the job was filled, and I had my own parish to serve. So I went back to Mount Hope, convinced that God was up to something but completely unsure of what to do with the experience.

Soon after that Sunday, I began to struggle in being in an all-white congregation. I began to feel dissatisfied and uncomfortable. Even though I loved being the pastor there and even though I loved the people tremendously, I no longer felt right serving in such a segregated environment. I felt the need to move on. So, I resigned and became a member of Beulah United Church of Christ, a small African American congregation near my home. And since I was feeling so restless and since college had been so traumatic for me, I decided to go back to school and study a topic that was fun, simply to take the opportunity to learn something new that was interesting to me. I enrolled at the North Carolina School of the Arts (NCSA), School of Filmmaking, in 1997 and began taking classes.

I had a great time. I laughed and fell in love with this institution that educates artists. I played and learned and worked on my craft of writing. It was here that I realized that writing fiction was really the thing I loved most. While I was in school, my friend left First Congregational and I applied for the position. In May of 1998, I was hired as the pastor. I left NCSA after a year and began focusing primarily on my writing and on my new pastorate. In July of 1998, *Friendship Cake* was sold. And now I have the incredible and blessed gift of doing two things that I love, being a pastor and a writer.

Being the white pastor of a predominantly African American church has brought extraordinary gifts into my life. I have never understood segregated worship among Christians. I have never felt at peace regarding issues of race in the South. I have always felt that people of faith, especially those of us who have greater privileges because of the color of our skin, need to do a better job of building bridges.

My life, my faith, my writing, and my ministry have all been influenced by the places I have worked, the people I have known. Hospice certainly taught me the most important lessons of life. I was shown love and the value of community at Mount Hope. I learned to celebrate the gifts of creativity and ministry from PSR and NCSA; and I have learned grace at First Congregational UCC. I have also had my eyes opened there. I have had to learn that racism is alive and well in North Carolina, in the educational system, in the medical care system, in the court system, and in the church. My hope is that by what the church and I are doing, by just being church together, we offer a model of hope and reconciliation to the rest of the world. And I must say it is by the church members' grace and God's goodness that I am able to serve them.

I recently turned forty and I spent a lot of time reflecting on my life, my ministry, and my faith. Across the years, it has become so clear to me that the hand of God has always been on me. It is not because I am special or different from any other child of God. It is certainly not because I am so faithful. It is only because of God's goodness.

I value that God has watched over me, guided me, and protected me, through good days and bad, in season and out of season. I took quite a few wrong turns, was denied access through some doors, failed and got up, stopped, moved backward, and sometimes stumbled forward. In spite of my wandering spirit and my disappointments and my failures, in spite of being told no so many times I can't even count them, in spite of being misunderstood and in spite of my misunderstanding, I know that God has always been with me. That God prepared a path for me, a path laden with sorrow as well as joy, with saints and with sinners, a path filled with stories to listen and to tell and a path requiring service; and that as long as I am attentive to God and that path, no matter what anyone else says about where I'm heading or no matter what stands in the way of my walking, I know that I will one day get home. As the old spiritual goes, "We've come this far by faith, leaning on the Lord; trusting in his holy word, he's never failed me yet. O can't turn around, we've come this far by faith."

Praise God for God's faithfulness. For God is good. All the time.

# CHARGE TO WOMANNESS

LYNNE HINTON

I know that it might make you blush
Me twirling in my purple dress
But that won't be enough to hush
My whirling womanness

It's the laughter from old Sarah
It's the tears in Rachel's eyes
It's the song and dance of Miriam
It's Rahab hiding spies

O the church may try to hide it
It may never be called blessed
But they cannot deny it
That bawdy womanness

That's what anointed Jesus
Bathed and kissed his feet
It touched the passing garment
Along a crowded street

It kept Mary at the cross
Magdaline never left his side
Womanness cradled Jesus
In her arms he died

So the world may laugh, may point, may stare
They may never let you rest
But they can't wipe away the past
Of our rooted womanness

It's all the colors of the rainbow
The vision in your clearest sight
The suffering heard though there're no words
The depth of your darkest night

It's that gnawing in your gut
That you cannot explain
It's the justice-seeking calling
To end another's pain

It may get you into trouble
It may make for you a mess
Though often it is silent
It's a living womanness

And when it's loud and screaming
And your heart begins to break
Hang on to your history
Live for your daughter's sake

You will often be misunderstood
They will put you to the test
But they can't take away
The power of womanness

It is courage; it is truth
It is you at your best
Praise God; be always faithful
to your womanness.

# GOD IS STILL SPEAKING: INSPIRED AND ENERGIZED BY POSSIBILITIES

NANCY PEELER KEPPEL

G od has called me so many times that I've thought of getting an unlisted number. The first few times I didn't recognize the voice. Sunday school teachers, male pastors, and Old Testament Bible stories had formed my image of God. He was an old man sitting on a throne in heaven. I was afraid of that faraway Father who knew my every thought and would punish me for breaking his commandments. I certainly couldn't imagine his getting in touch with me. One of God's first calls came in the voice of a friend.

Mary Ellen Trivette asked if I would be willing to take a carload of Methodists to a silent retreat at Church of the Savior in Washington, D.C. I didn't know anything about silent retreats, but it sounded good to me because, even though I was forty years old, it took all the courage I could muster just to say my name in front of a group. "Sure, I'll do that," I said, "When do we leave?" Mary Ellen gave me directions to a church near Hickory, North Carolina, and asked me to be there at 6:00 the next morning.

Our retreat was at Day Spring, a beautiful setting on the outskirts of Washington, D.C. After three days of silence, even during meals, the sixteen retreatants sat in a circle on the floor of a rustic lodge and talked about spiritual gifts. That was a new concept for me. I knew about talents—musical, artistic, writing, oratory, etc.—and I knew I didn't have any of those. I listened as each person's gift was identified and celebrated as a call to ministry. When my turn came, I was mortified at the thought of being the only one without talents or gifts. Everyone looked at me and then one by one they all said, "Nancy, you are a good listener."

Soon after I returned home a second call came through Emily Lester, a laywoman in the United Church of Christ. She invited me to a workshop on lay ministry at the Blowing Rock Assembly Grounds. It was there that I came to understand another terminology and theology, one that identified laypeople as ministers. Because I had thought of ministers only as ordained males, it took a while to come to terms with the implication that I had spiritual gifts and that God was calling me to use them in ministry. When I was a child, I experienced the minister at St. John's Lutheran Church in Salisbury, North Carolina, as pious and distant, a teacher with all the answers. It never occurred to me to question anything he said or to ask questions of my own. He led worship and preached on Sunday, taught the catechism classes, baptized babies, served communion, and officiated at funerals. I didn't want to do any of those things. So as I became aware of my spiritual gifts: encouragement, availability, acceptance, love of God and people, plus my listening skills, I needed to come up with a way to respond to God's call that was different from the traditional pastor's role.

Our family had moved to Hickory, North Carolina, in 1960 and joined Corinth United Church of Christ, the home church of my brother-in-law, Robert Moss, who became president of the denomination in 1969. He and his wife, Junia, were not only great friends but also prophetic, faithful, and loving Christians who served as my mentors. They encouraged and supported me as I struggled to determine my part in God's mission for the world.

In 1964 I realized that I had became so thoroughly immersed in my role as mother of three children that I had little time or concern for anything else. Nothing was more important than their happiness and well-being. They had become idols. I worshiped them.

Then one autumn day my twenty-month-old daughter, Jane, ran a high fever and screamed in pain when I touched her. I put her on a large pillow and took her to our pediatrician. As he examined her, I noticed that her skin came off on his fingers. Alarmed, he called in his partner. After exchanging a few whispered words, they asked me to take Jane home. They promised to talk with her father, a doctor, about the diagnosis.

I later realized that they couldn't bear to tell me that our daughter had a horrible disease that was rare and had no known treatment. Only thirty-three cases of toxic epidermal necrolysis had been reported at that time. About half of those people afflicted had died within a week. Others were left blind. Jane's flesh peeled, seeped, and had a terrible odor. It was as if she had third-degree burns over her entire body. We could not put any clothing on her and she drank fluids through a straw.

Because of the danger of infection, we kept her at home. She lay naked in her crib. I told her stories, read nursery rhymes, and sang to her. I stayed in her room day and night for a week. She showed no signs of improvement. On the seventh day, I left the room. I lay on my bed and sobbed. Through my tears, I thanked God for the short time this precious child was ours and acknowledged that it was time to let her go. Then I began planning her funeral.

Within hours, Jane began to improve. Slowly, over the next several months, her hair grew back, her skin healed, and she learned to walk again. She became the vivacious, healthy, happy child we had known.

That near-death experience changed profoundly my understanding of the nature of God. I experienced God's love as so much greater than my own and became certain that no matter what happened, God would be listening to my prayers, giving me guidance, strength, and the peace that passes all understanding. From the time of Jane's healing until this day, I have never doubted God's loving presence.

This traumatic experience sensitized me to the profound grief being experienced by people in our congregation and in our community as their loved ones were dying. I heard Elisabeth Kübler-Ross speak, I read books, visited the nursing homes, and met with Jean Settlemeyer, the hospital administrator, to ask if we could start a hospice in our town. She made it happen. I helped with the volunteer training and for several years was a volunteer myself.

A natural extension of that ministry was to train peer counselors at Lenoir Rhyne College. One of the students told me that there were classmates coming back to school after going home for a family member's funeral and they had no one to talk with. The teachers, unaware of the situation, couldn't understand why they were behind in their work. That conversation led me to start a grief support group for those who had lost a loved one and for the peer counselors who wanted to help them through that difficult time.

When Martin Luther King was assassinated, I asked to put flowers on the altar in his memory. Our pastor not only denied my request but also didn't even mention the tragic event in the worship service. It was a wake-up call for me. I realized that no black people were seen at our church except for the "maid" and janitor and that our kindergarten classes had no children of color. I began noticing other things that didn't seem right at the church. The entire "ruling" body was made up of men—deacons, elders, and the consistory president, the pastor. It was always the women who were in the kitchen cooking for the brotherhood meetings and other activities; children weren't allowed to play on the grass or in the fellowship hall; the language used in worship, hymnals, and reports was sexist; and pregnant women were asked to stop processing with the choir (me included).

With the hope of righting some of these wrongs, I volunteered for the pastor search committee in 1968. Gordon Sperry was called and he shared my concerns about the racist climate, the sexist policies, and the need for more involvement of the laity. In September 1970, I offered my services as a full-time volunteer staff member, without a "call" from the congregation, a job description, a title, or a salary. I just showed up and went to work. It was what I wanted to do and what I felt God was asking me to do.

My "office" was a metal desk in a corner of the church parlor. I had a telephone and a manual typewriter. My high school typing course was probably the most important course I had in all my years of schooling. Those were the days of carbon paper and duplicating machines.

I got my name back. Everybody called me Nancy instead of Mrs. Keppel, Mrs. Doctor Keppel, the doctor's wife, Mr. Peeler's daughter, Tim, Ken, and Jane's mother. I became a person in my own right, apart from the roles I played.

There was much debate among the male clergy before they voted to allow me to be a member of the UCC Catawba District Minister's Association. They had never before considered an unpaid, unordained, unmale person for membership in their elite group. Soon after I was officially included, I received an unsolicited brochure promoting an "ethnetics" (race relations) workshop led by a Raleigh man named Mac Hulslander. At that time, there was considerable racial tension in the schools and in the community at large. I suggested that we have a retreat for our ministerial group and invite Mac to be our leader. They agreed. I picked up Mac at the Hickory bus station and we drove together to the Blowing Rock Assembly Grounds. That was the beginning of a relationship that led eventually to the formation of CLAY: Clergy and Laity Together in Ministry, an ecumenical organization that will celebrate its twenty-fifth anniversary in 2003. The "Faith to Focused Ministry" program proved life changing for many participants from diverse faith perspectives and continues to be a valuable resource for the understanding of call and for ministry "in, through, and beyond the local congregation."

Mac and I wrote the UCC pronouncement on "Empowering the Laity for Ministry" in 1975 and shepherded it through the Southern Conference and the 13th General Synod that passed it in 1981. We promoted lay ministry with workshops at Duke Divinity School, Lancaster Seminary, Lenoir Rhyne College, at every Southern Conference event that would give us a platform, and in local congregations.

In February 1971, I was named Parish Worker at Corinth. In October 1974, the consistory voted to compensate me for two-thirds of my time with a salary of $5,000 annually (no benefits). I was given a job description based on the work I had done over my four volunteer years.

## JOB DESCRIPTION: PARISH WORKER

I. She shall work toward coordinating meetings and activities of the consistory, boards, organizations, committees and groups of the congregation and community to promote harmony in scheduling, use of facilities, equipment, and resources.

2. She shall work closely with the staff and boards in planning and promoting the church's ministry to adults through group activities, recreation, discussions, service projects, and retreats.

3. She shall have staff responsibility for the Women's Guild and for outreach to visitors and potential new members through regular and organized visitation, selected mailings, telephone follow-up, and maintaining of potential members files. She shall have staff responsibilities with the Board of Kindergarten Education, the Congregational Life Board, and work closely with the evangelism committee.

4. She shall recruit members of the congregation to serve as official hosts for church families and guests at times of weddings, funerals, receptions, concerts, conferences, and meetings.

5. She shall discover, announce, and promote leadership and growth opportunities such as conferences, workshops, and retreats which may be available locally, within the conference and association, or nationally. She shall relate the results of these meetings to the needs of our congregation.

IN ADDITION, SHE SHALL:

1. Prepare and distribute the *Direct Line,* the monthly newsletter. 2. Prepare the church's annual report. 3. Assist the pastor in visitation as assigned. 4. Procure curriculum materials, supplies, etc. and promote the use of bulletin boards, display areas, etc. 5. Coordinate special activities such as Laity Sunday, One Great Hour of Sharing, family nights, seasonal activities, summer camping, etc. 6. Plan and coordinate the annual August Adventures or similar summer programs.

Encouraged by my clergywomen friends, I applied twice for certification in Christian education by the Division of Christian Education, Board of Homeland Ministries. The first time I was rejected because "certification is for persons employed professionally in Church Education, not for volunteers, even full-time ones. Think what would happen to the quality of medical care if there were not rigorous licensing procedures for doctors." The fact that I was a certified teacher in North Carolina and had taught at Duke University and in the Georgia public schools didn't matter. The second time I was rejected because I did not have a seminary degree. By that time I had been to conferences, courses, lectures, workshops, etc. and had gotten an education in organizational development, role of women in church and society, experiential theology, journaling, conflict utilization, case study method, spiritual growth, drug counseling, stewardship and evangelism, death and dying, divorce and marriage counseling, human sexuality, singles ministry, prayer, chancel drama, personal growth, career and life planning, transactional analysis, church consulting, and other areas of interest to me.

Ironically, I received a letter two years later asking me to apply for certification. That was followed by a request from the Office for Church Life and Leadership to write a paper on "Celebrating People's Ministries." In 1975, the Western North Carolina Association at its annual meeting recognized me as a Commissioned Minister. This status is given to laypersons in specific church-related service.

My life changed the night of our older son's high school graduation when my husband moved out of our home. We had been happily married for over twenty years. The only explanation I received was "you are not the same person I married." "Halleluiah!" I said. "Goodbye," he said. After the obligatory North Carolina waiting period, we were divorced and he remarried. I stayed in our house with the three children. Being single again, I could better empathize with the struggles of single women and men. I, also, had more time to give to other areas of ministry.

God continued to give me opportunities plus another gift, the courage to speak out on controversial issues. I initiated the formation of a NOW chapter, the Catawba County Woman's Task Force, the Woman's Resource Exchange, an integrated kindergarten, a Sunday church school class for mentally challenged children, a singles' ecumenical Sunday school class that rotated among four churches, and a support group for single-again women. I started a Good Samaritan fund for people in need, invited patients from Broughton Psychiatric Hospital to come to Corinth for lunch and fellowship, and worked with Corinth's Saturday Stewards in refurbishing houses and providing other services in the community. I served on Hickory's Human Relations Council for six years and became an active member of the NAACP. I am now a life member of that important organization.

I managed to generate hate mail when *The Hickory Daily Record* quoted me on gun control. "It bothers me that our taxes support classes at the police department where young people and women are taught to handle guns. I wish these people and the rest of the community were being schooled in the development of good human relations. I would support anything that would get rid of guns. I could say a lot more, but I'm afraid someone might shoot me." One angry man wrote, "You know about as much as a child about guns. Common sense (which you undoubtly [*sic*] lack) is all that is needed to know that all you are after is publicity. Human relations is not helped by your dumb remarks."

Another avenue of ministry began on a dark, rainy morning when a neighbor going through an ugly divorce called to ask if he could come to my house at noon to talk. I said, "Sure," and invited him to have a sandwich with me. Neither of us had a bite to eat before he grabbed me, dragged me to my bedroom, and sexually assaulted me. I couldn't talk about what happened for three years. During those years, I listened to the stories of other women who had been traumatized in similar and different situations. I started a support group for them (and me). Together we formed a county Rape Crisis Task Force with a hotline staffed by volunteers.

My understanding of ministry was enhanced in the summer of 1976. For as long as I could remember, I had wanted to go to Africa, not as a tourist, but to live among the people. After my divorce, I had that chance. Trudy and Dick Braun, United Church of Christ medical missionaries in Ghana, invited me to live and work with them for a month in a Schweitzer-like hospital in Adidome, a small village located two hours northeast of Accra, the capital and port city. Dick was the hospital's surgeon, general practitioner, and medical superintendent.

Trudy was the matron of the hospital. She was nurse, teacher, "mother," and friend of the whole community. It was truly an outward-bound experience. I traveled alone and out of the States for the first time in my life. It was a time of military coups, severe drought, shortages of gas, food, water, and medical supplies. I learned to appreciate a bath in the river, an orange, a hard wooden bench to sit on for the three-hour church services, African music, dance, and art. But most of all I appreciated and came to love the faithful, cheerful, friendly people who welcomed me into their lives.

My son, Ken, gave me a book one Christmas that inspired me to begin a whole new ministry. It was William Glasser's *Reality Therapy*. I had been using my listening skills in informal counseling and decided to get some training that would make me a better counselor. I attended conferences, lectures, workshops, and read all of Dr. Glasser's books for two years. Then in 1978, I went to Ladycliffe College in New York State for the first week of training. That was followed by supervision and a second training session a year later. In 1980, I went to California and was certified as a reality therapist by the Institute of Reality Therapy. I taught graduate students, clergy, parents, children (my own included) to use this counseling method, and I welcomed as counselees anyone who seemed interested in the concept of responsibility for one's own decisions and chosen behavior. I have never accepted any remuneration for this ministry.

I know my limitations and so I don't hesitate to ask anyone to use her or his gifts in ministry. Success has most often occurred when I stayed in the background and encouraged and supported the gifted women and men who always seemed ready to participate in God's mission and to provide the necessary maintenance to keep the ministry alive. My dad who worked at the same job for seventy years told me that my "problem" is that I never stick with anything. It is true. I am always drawn to something new. I am inspired and energized by possibilities.

At the conclusion of the Southern Conference meeting in 1977, I went to the microphone and asked anyone who was interested in forming a Task Force for Women to come speak with me. Cally Rogers-Witte, a volunteer staff member of Community Church in Chapel Hill, was the first to express her enthusiasm and several other women followed. After months of corresponding with other UCC task forces and members of the national staff, we held our first meeting of the "Task Force for Women in Church and Society" at the Southern Conference office in Graham, North Carolina. Our purpose was to "advocate the equal partnership of women with men at all levels of church life." We introduced a resolution at the 1982 annual meeting of the Southern Conference urging ratification of the equal rights amendment; we encouraged churches to allow women in their pulpits; and we submitted a resolution on inclusive language that was studied and implemented in the Conference. We traveled throughout North Carolina and eastern Virginia doing workshops for clergy titled "You Too Can Be a Feminist," and we challenged sexism and racism at every opportunity. The complete history of the Woman's Task Force is in the library at Elon University.

My efforts to promote peace and justice were enhanced by participation in an organization I helped found in Hickory. It was named "Peace Is Possible." We held seminars, developed educational materials, mailed out newsletters monthly, and kept informed on public policies. The two conflicts with Iraq, the Middle East crisis, and conflicts worldwide in recent years have provided many more opportunities for peacemaking.

My official position at Corinth ended with a phone call from the Consistory president. I answered the call at a reality-therapy training session in New York State. She said, "We have voted to do away with your position. Do you have any questions?" I didn't ask questions then and I wasn't given a chance to ask any later. I can't say that I was too surprised. Two weeks earlier I had written a letter to the consistory asking that I be given a leave of absence until the congregation reinstated its contributions to Our Church World Missions (OCWM), supported our national church leaders, and understood the justice issues explicit in the UCC's support of Ben Chavis and the Wilmington Ten.

When I returned to Hickory and Corinth from New York, I continued most of what I had been doing, again on a volunteer basis. I began working on getting the OCWM money back in the budget. I found members who were willing to join me in a telephone campaign explaining the importance of supporting the United Church of Christ. A congregational meeting followed this. We had counted our votes carefully and the OCWM money was reinstated. I learned a valuable lesson from this experience: never call for a vote until you are certain of the outcome.

In 1984, I moved to Raleigh and bought a four-bedroom house so that my women friends running for the state legislature could live with me while the General Assembly was in session. They were good Democrats and were all defeated that fall in a Republican sweep. So I made the extra bedrooms available for rent to men and women who needed a temporary home. My basement became a storage place for anyone who needed space to store her or his household goods and personal belongings. One woman on food stamps, who had to leave North Carolina in order to avoid paying child support to her lawyer husband, came back eight years later to reclaim her treasures.

My older son, Tim, played a big part in the direction of my ministry during my first years in Raleigh. He was working for the Catholic diocese in the Peace and Justice division and got me involved in ministry around the death penalty and Central America. I became active in North Carolinians Against the Death Penalty, Witness for Peace, and CITCA (Carolina Interfaith Task Force on Central America). When Contras kidnapped Tim in 1985, I really had my consciousness raised about the role of the United States in promoting death and destruction in Nicaragua. I participated in protest demonstrations. I wrote letters to the editors, to legislators, to all my friends, and learned all I could about Central America. I attended worship services and prayer vigils. I marched in Washington, Raleigh, and Blacksburg, Virginia. I committed myself to change U.S. policy and rejoiced when the war ended.

God works in mysterious ways. I had never heard the term "sexual orientation." I didn't know any gay people, or so I thought. I was ignorant of any problems that they faced, and I am probably in the 100-percentile category of heterosexuals. I could never have imagined that God would call me to this ministry. This is what happened. I had been living in Raleigh for about three years. My counselor and friend, Mahan Siler, had become the pastor at Pullen Memorial Baptist Church shortly before I moved from Hickory. It was at Pullen that I met the Reverend June Norris, pastor of the Metropolitan Community Church that shared facilities with Community UCC, my church home. She was part of a panel discussion on homosexuality. It was enlightening and extremely disturbing.

Soon after that discussion, I was appointed to the Raleigh Human Resources/Human Relations Commission (HRHRAC). As a representative of that group, I was invited by the Reverend Jim Lewis to a meeting at the Episcopal Diocese to discuss ways to make our capital city a safer and happier place for the homosexual community. The decision was made to have a public hearing in the city council chambers. I coordinated efforts with HRHRAC members to sponsor the hearing. Most of the speakers told their own stories of terror, pain, and sorrow. I invited Mahan to speak from the point of view of a non-gay pastor. His stirring speech had a profound effect on everyone. He empathized with the suffering people and he took responsibility for himself and religious bodies for adding to that suffering.

After the hearing, I had conversations with my pastor, Cally Rogers-Witte, Morris Hudgins (Unitarian Universalist), Jim Lewis (Episcopal), Mahan Siler (Southern Baptist), Charlie Mulholland (Catholic), and Jimmy Creech (United Methodist) about forming a group to look at possible plans of action. As a group, we decided to have a conference that included all faith communities. I invited pastors from Metropolitan Community Church, the Jewish synagogue, Shaw Divinity School, and Presbyterian and Lutheran churches to join in this effort. In the last six months of 1987, a close-knit group of religious leaders emerged in Raleigh, united by a determination to assure equality to gay men, lesbians, and bisexual persons. The Raleigh Religious Network for Gay and Lesbian Equality (RRNGLE) was born! It was a miracle brought about by divine intervention and providential circumstances.

Membership was open to anyone who wanted to join; there were no dues and no official structure. Monthly breakfast meetings, held at various churches, were a joyous occasion. We became a powerful community of best friends. For eight years, conferences were held annually and attracted gay and nongay, clergy and laity alike to seriously confront injustice and to worship together as God's children. The City of Raleigh passed a nondiscrimination ordinance based on sexual orientation, the first by a capital city in the South. Other similar networks were formed across the state, and lives were changed. Families were reunited, doors were opened, and God poured blessings of love, understanding, and acceptance on all of us.

Dave Barber, my Community UCC pastor in 1991, called to ask me if I was interested in sex. "Is that an invitation?" I joked. I knew that he had suggested that I represent the Conference at a training session in New York to introduce the UCC's program for mission: "Created in God's Image." Our church was one of nine churches to test this program. I served as coordinator, and two other lay members of our congregation led the sessions. It was one of the most rewarding experiences of my ministry. Dave, Robin J. Townsley Arcus, and I became a team and trained many members of churches throughout the Southern Conference to use this valuable resource.

I first learned about Habitat for Humanity when I was in Ghana, and I supported it with an interest-free loan when I returned to the States. When I moved to Raleigh, I became aware of the good work being done locally and decided to suggest that Community UCC consider sponsoring a house. They agreed. Then I met with the pastors of Pullen Memorial Baptist Church, Laodicea UCC, and Martin Street Baptist Church and proposed that they join us in this venture. Together these four congregations built a house. It was the first partnership across racial and interdenominational lines in Raleigh.

I continue to write letters to the editor. The most recent expressed an alternative to a state lottery, my concern over the method of spent nuclear waste storage at the Sherwin-Harris nuclear plant, and my opposition to a war with Iraq. I'm also giving commentaries on WUNC radio, our local NPR station in Chapel Hill on many different topics. My ability to do this has come as a complete surprise.

In May 2001, at age 71, I was diagnosed with breast cancer. I had a lumpectomy followed by seven weeks of radiation treatment. This "bump in the road" was followed by a diagnosis of bone cancer in January of 2003 that necessitated radiation and chemotherapy. I moved to Blacksburg, Virginia, to receive treatment and to be near my daughter and her family. I am working on a project that will contain the inspiring stories of laypeople who have answered God's call.

Thank goodness, God did not call me to be a pastor. I could never have survived the challenges, tribulations, and constraints of that specialized ministry. I continue to be inspired and energized by possibilities. I don't know what the future holds, but I do know that God is still speaking and that I am still listening.

# QUERY OF CHILD PERTINENT

**Letter to the Editor, *The Hickory Daily Record***

🔳

NANCY PEELER KEPPEL

*To the editor:*

The N.C. General Assembly met August 20, 1920, with the opportunity to become the 36th state to ratify a proposed constitutional amendment which reads, "The right of citizens of the U.S. to vote shall not be denied or abridged by the United States or by any state on account of sex."

The House of Representatives failed to ratify. It was over 50 years later, in 1971, that the N.C. General Assembly finally ratified the 19th constitutional amendment which gave women the right to vote.

The N.C. General Assembly meeting in June 1982 had the opportunity to become the 36th state to ratify a proposed 27th constitutional amendment which reads "Equality of rights under law shall not be denied or abridged by the U.S. or by any state on account of sex."

On June 4, 1982, an un-holy alliance of 27 senators met in the Senate chapel and vowed to table the ERA, thereby eliminating the possibility for open discussion, debate, and vote on the amendment.

Once again, North Carolina legislators have denied U.S. citizens basic human, democratic, and legal rights. It is a tragedy that history now records that North Carolina was among the minority of states that failed to ratify the ERA!

A special word of appreciation to Sen. Cass Ballenger. I was one of the naïve voters who believed that elected officials voted the will of their constituents—you taught me the fallacy of that belief. I will never again be quite so naïve when I go to the polls.

After the Raleigh rally on June 6, I went to a restaurant with my family. There I met a 9-year-old girl, her hair in pigtails. She looked at my green ERA-Yes buttons and white dress, then said: "You must be for the Equal Rights Amendment. Did you go to the rally?" I answered, "Yes, did you?" "No," she said, "I couldn't go because I had a softball game. We got creamed, as usual. I probably couldn't have gotten anyone to take me, anyway. I have real dumb relatives who don't believe in equal rights." Then very tentatively she asked, "Have we ever had equal rights?" I answered, "No," "Will we ever have them?" she wanted to know. Who will answer this child?

*Used by permission of the artist.*

# WOMEN IN CHURCH AND SOCIETY TASK FORCE

## Annual Report by Task Force Chair, June 1982

NANCY PEELER KEPPEL

The purpose of this Task Force is to "advocate the equal partnership of women with men at all levels of the church life." In order to achieve this goal we have been guided by ten objectives. In some areas of concern we have seen real progress. In others we have made only a small beginning.

We addressed our priority issues—racism and sexism—at the workshop held at Crumpton Center in Roxboro. Dr. Marion Blair led us through a study and worship experience which enlightened and enriched us.

A retreat for women in ministry was sponsored by the School of Pastoral Care and Jeanette Stokes' Resource Center for Women. I enjoyed serving on the planning committee.

The election of all male officers of the Southern Conference was protested at the 1981 annual meeting.

A letter was sent to the Search Committee encouraging the selection of a Conference Minister sensitive to the needs and concerns of women.

In keeping with our ongoing commitment to equality, the Task Force will introduce a resolution at the 1982 Annual meeting urging ratification of the Equal Rights Amendment by the N. C. legislature before the June 30 deadline.

Members of the Task Force believe the Christian Gospel urges us to make this witness. We know that in Christ there is neither Jew nor Greek, bond nor free, male nor female. Church people can avoid responding to this truth, but we cannot deny the truth.

The Amendment reads as follows:

Section 1. Equality of rights under the law shall not be denied or abridged by the United States or by any State on account of sex.

Section 2. The Congress shall have the power to enforce, by appropriate legislation, the provisions of this article.

Section 3. This amendment shall take effect two years after the date of ratification.

As is our policy, individual Task Force members do their "work" between meetings by being actively involved in justice issues in their churches and communities. Fran Carnright, Forest Wells, Susie Keele, Jill Edens, Winfred Bray, Dot Ballinger, Gail Hooper, and John Kernodle are "doing theology" and effecting change in attitudes and circumstances. We are grateful for their insight, energy, courage, and their commitment to servanthood in Christ's name.

*The Southern Conference News,* June 1982, p. 14.

# WOMEN IN CHURCH AND SOCIETY TASK FORCE

## Annual Report by Task Force Chair, June 1983

▦

NANCY PEELER KEPPEL

Over the past eight years the Task Force on Women in Church and Society has served The Southern Conference by identifying and responding to theological and social issues related particularly to women.

This year we were encouraged by our closer association with Southern Conference Church Women. We presented a workshop at Summer Conference, led worship at WNC Fall Enrichment, provided inclusive language worship materials, reported at the executive meeting in Durham, and were involved in other ways through our three association Task Forces.

Our ties to the Southern Conference were strengthened when I was invited to report to the board of directors. We are looking forward to working with a Conference Staff intern who will coordinate women's ministry. Clergy women were invited to meet with us in April so that we could learn how to better support them.

Our relationship with women throughout the denomination has been enhanced because of our membership in UCC Women in Mission.

As members of the Task Force we have grown in our understanding of racism and sexism. We have studied and worked hard on breaking down barriers which prevent minorities and women from participating fully in the Church and in the world.

We have taken a few steps forward but are sad to report that at this point in our history:

In our church:

All Southern Conference staff ministers are male.

All Southern Conference officers are male.

All Commission Coordinators are male.

All Southern Conference institutions are headed by males.

All Southern Conference institution boards are chaired by males.

Only a few of our ordained female clergy have been called to serve as pastors of a church.

Our language is exclusive, especially in worship.

In our world:

Our constitution does not have an Equal Rights Amendment.

Women earn approximately 60% of what men earn.

Two out of three older Americans living in poverty are women.

Men receive 90% of the world's income and own 99% of all property.

Reproductive freedom is in jeopardy.

Gender discrimination exists in education, insurance plans, industry, and media.

Incidences of spouse abuse (physical) occur in over 50% of marriages.

One out of every three women will be victims of rape or attempted rape during their lifetime (according to Rape Crisis Center in Washington, DC).

And so the challenge is there for the Task Force to continue to open eyes, ears, and hearts to the victims of sexism and racism: to correct the injustice which permeates our world. We are committed to that struggle. But we need the support of all our brothers and sisters. Together we can make a difference.

*The Southern Conference News,* June 1983, p. 14.

# MANY WATERS

DENISE CUMBEE LONG

[Yahweh] will come to us like the showers,
like the spring rains that water the earth.

HOSEA 6:3

The first memory I have of an encounter with God occurred when I was seven, standing in a light spring rain at the end of the garden path near our home in St. Andrews, Scotland. I remember walking to the rose bed near the back of the stone wall, which fenced this typically British garden. For some reason, I felt a need to walk alone to this beautiful spot and look up at the gray sky. The mist dampened my serious face. I wondered about God. *I will remember this,* I thought. And, somehow, this memory has indeed stayed with me throughout my life, attached to all the sights, sounds, and smells that accompanied it. God came to me as a warm rain in the spring of my life, and I have found her in the form of many waters since then.

I am the oldest child of a mother and father who both attended seminary. I grew up in a household in which institutional and academic religion were part of our family life. Both of my parents were from southern families who had instilled in them the values of hard work, the importance of family ties, and the centrality of the church in daily life. However, both my mother and father were unlike their families of origin in their views on the social and political issues of the time. I grew up with a sense of the importance of social justice and an appreciation for diversity. I also learned that religion was used to justify both the liberation and oppression of people, and that it could be a divisive issue in larger family gatherings.

I was born in Winston-Salem, but my family left North Carolina shortly afterward. My father pastored small churches in Florida and Virginia during my first five years of life, then he moved our family to Scotland while he completed a Ph.D. in pastoral counseling at St. Mary's College. In 1966, he accepted a position on the faculty at Bangor Theological Seminary in Bangor, Maine. We sailed back to the States in the Queen Elizabeth and settled into a large Victorian house on the campus of the seminary.

Soon, we joined the American Baptist church in town. It was the place we went every Sunday, and there was no question of doing otherwise. My friends were there. Adults were kind and tolerant of childish horseplay. The traditional God with white robes and a kingly countenance became an image at the fringe of my life. God was there, but remote, like the adults at church. He was unquestionably male, and he did not have much to do with me.

> [Yahweh] leads me beside still waters;
> [Yahweh] restores my soul.
>
> PSALM 23:2-3

One of the best things my parents did when we moved to Maine was to buy a cottage on a glacial lake about an hour from Bangor. Every summer, when school was out, we moved out to this woodsy retreat, and my father would commute into work every day. My brother, sisters, and I spent hours swimming in the clear, cold waters of Branch Lake, and I fell asleep at night listening to the call of loons. The lake was my energy, my creativity, and my refuge. It was my connection with the divine force that moves through all things. When I was upset, I would run down to the end of the dock and dive into the water, washing away the sadness for a while. When I was angry, I would swim furiously as far off shore as I dared. My sister and I would play a game in which we would challenge each other to find a white rock thrown by the other into deeper and deeper water. I remember swimming down, down, toward the shining stone gleaming like a light amidst the rocks and sand at the bottom and clutching it in triumphant fingers as I rose with bursting lungs to the surface again. This was a time of diving and surfacing, of growing up, of soaking up sun on warm, rough boulders, of turning brown and sprouting breasts, of reading *The Chronicles of Narnia* and imagining God as the wild and beautiful Aslan.

For the first time, I began to think of God in metaphors that were more appealing to my young, romantic mind. The lake itself took on a sheen of divinity. It was a constant presence but constantly changing, sometimes smooth as glass, sometimes stirred into ripples by a breeze, sometimes lashed into small waves by a storm. It surrounded me with a cleansing energy, teased me with hidden treasures, beckoned me to leave the stability of earth and leap into its mysterious depths. It could be as transparent as glass or as dark as a night sky. Mostly, it was life, and God lived beneath its depths, hovered over its surface, and broke apart in the white birch trees that edged the shore. I was a pure pantheist, though I could never have named it as such.

[She] is like a tree
planted by streams of water.

PSALM 1:3, adapted

I did well in school, and teachers encouraged me to think about my future. I had no idea what I wanted to be or do. There were too many options, too many courses of study. I liked all of them. My parents urged me to consider any career I wanted. I read a biography of Albert

Schweitzer, a man who combined a love of theology and music with radical service. If he could do it all, then so could I. I would go to medical school and become a doctor in Africa or India.

My family moved from Maine back to the South, and I started college at Wake Forest University. A child of Southern Baptists, it was natural for me to attend a college with that heritage, at least so my parents thought. I quickly gave up my premed studies after a rocky semester of math and science and gravitated toward literature, philosophy, and religion. The summer after my freshman year, I worked as a youth director in a rural church in the foothills of North Carolina. At the orientation, I met a fellow student who was also doing a summer internship in a small church about an hour away. I was eighteen, he was twenty, and we were in love. We found ourselves in many of the same philosophy and religion classes back at Wake Forest and quickly became inseparable. A week after I graduated, Doug Long and I were married.

We both attended Southeastern Baptist Theological Seminary, Doug because he had known from the age of nine that he wanted to be a minister, and I because I didn't know what I wanted to do, and it was the path of least resistance. I really didn't picture myself as a pastor. However, I loved all the theology classes, be it systematic, process, or narrative. Philosophy of religion and Old Testament courses were also favorites. I began to imagine finishing seminary, getting a graduate degree, and teaching at a college or divinity school. But, toward the end of that first year, I became bothered by the nagging thought that academia might prove to be an ivory tower existence. I did not want to isolate myself from the rough-and-tumble real world where struggling for justice and working for systemic change did not require theological training. Once again I tried a "let's see what happens if I apply" approach. I took the LSAT and applied to UNC-Chapel Hill School of Law. To my surprise, I was accepted and given scholarships and loans to attend. So, I backed into the legal arena, wondering what I might do with a law degree if I were to actually finish.

I quickly discovered that I hated law school. The classes were dry, technical, and geared to those who were interested in private or corporate practice. I jumped ship after a year and headed back to Southeastern to finish my master's of divinity. Seminary proved to be an affirmation of my preaching gifts. I was chosen for one of the coveted student preaching slots at weekly chapel service. While nine months pregnant, I finished a summer school preaching class with flying colors, even though I had to sit on a barstool to deliver my sermons to the class because my swollen ankles couldn't take twenty minutes of my unmoving weight. Still, I could not picture myself in a pastoral role. Postponing a career by attending school was an attractive option.

As Doug and I finished our seminary degrees, we were saddened and angered by the creeping fundamentalism that was infecting Southeastern and other Southern Baptist institutions at the time. We realized that we did not want to spend our time fighting like salmon against the current with a denomination that, for the most part, did not share our social or theological outlook. After looking around for a better denominational "fit," we settled on the United Church of Christ, which was like a breath of fresh air. On the national level, it was known for progressive stances on many social issues. On the local level, the Eastern North Carolina Association of the Southern Conference, we found it to be refreshingly racially diverse. Although Doug and I soon discovered that a small-town UCC congregation could be just as conservative as the Baptist or Methodist church down the street, we still felt an overall sense of kinship and belonging as we both became ordained UCC clergy.

After Doug accepted a position with a UCC congregation in Burlington, North Carolina, I decided to finish my law school degree at Chapel Hill. Our daughter, Jessica, was not yet two, and our son, Jordan, was barely four months old. We bought some land bordering the Haw River and built a small house. My days were filled with children, church, and reading case law on the deck looking over the field sloping to the river. I was happy in the rhythms of work and family life. The elusive and perfect career could wait.

But let justice roll down like waters,
and righteousness like an everflowing stream.

AMOS 5:24

I finished law school in 1988. Now, I had two graduate degrees and still no clue about what I wanted to do. Working for a couple of area law firms made it clear that I did not like traditional legal practice. It simply did not speak to my creative self. Also, I discovered to my chagrin that a law degree really didn't prepare one for cutting edge social justice work. So, I accepted a part-time position on the staff of the Southern Conference of the United Church of Christ with the title of program associate for Christian social ministries.

I was hired by Dr. Rollin Russell, then Conference minister, to take on a new staff role of connecting UCC congregations to social justice ministries on a local or national level. I flung myself into this position with relish, setting up bus trips to Washington, D.C. for Southern Conference folk to participate in marches against South African apartheid, organizing educational tours of community action groups working in triracial Robeson County, and planning a forum in which pro-life and pro-choice laity and clergy could come together for dialogue. I was naïve about denominational politics and church diplomacy, but very enthusiastic, and the varied menu of activism, preaching, writing for publications, and administrative work was quite appealing. However, I still found myself hungering for an international experience. The Albert Schweitzer role model continued to be my ideal of how one should live and work in the world.

> For [Yahweh] your God is bringing you into a good land,
> a land with flowing streams, with springs and
> underground waters welling up in valleys and hills.
>
> DEUTERONOMY 8:7

In 1991, Doug and I decided to leave our jobs in Burlington and travel to rural Mexico to live and work for a year as International Partners with Habitat for Humanity. Living in a rural village in the Puebla-Veracruz region was an experience that changed my life. Our family moved into a small cinder-block house in the pueblo of La Union de Zihuateutla. Tropical plants covered the mountains around us. Everything was moist and green. Banana trees grew beside our house. We had no mail service, telephone, doctor, or grocery store. Drinking water was secured from a spring at the top of a nearby hill, which we then boiled. I learned to speak some basic Spanish, wash clothes in a stone sink, and cook a chicken with the head and claws still attached.

We were supposed to provide technical assistance to a local Habitat for Humanity project, but soon found that we were the real students.

My eyes were opened to a new reality in which I was confronted for the first time with an entirely different worldview and life experience that was as valid as mine, and probably more authentic. The campesino men and women who became our friends were courageous, articulate, and deeply compassionate. Many were indigenous Totonaco, who spoke a soft language filled with gentle clicks and whispered sibilants. The community meetings were lessons in true democracy as women and men, young and old, stood to share their views with respectful tones. Our children played with tiny boys and girls who were the same age but half their size. We left Mexico after a year, feeling an immense gratitude for the privilege of that experience, and determined to keep "The Mexican Connection" alive in whatever future ministries we chose.

> Everyone who thirsts,
> come to the waters.
>
> ISAIAH 55:1

Upon returning to the States, we rented a house in Burlington and threw our resumes to the winds. I again worked with a local law firm while we contemplated where we would go next. I was surprised that I made it to the final interviews for a position with the national UCC offices in Cleveland, which encompassed community organizing. But, in the end, Doug was offered a plum pastorate at a historically liberal congregation in Oberlin, Ohio, and we moved there in 1992. First Church in Oberlin was a community of faith with a rich history of almost 150 years of social activism. From its role in the abolitionist movement and as a safe haven on the Underground Railroad, to its advocacy for civil rights, women's rights, and the inclusion of gay and lesbian members, First Church exemplified the best of an older, liberal church. I liked the other-directed nature of this congregation. A sense of being of service to the community was apparent in the very name that was used for the main worship building. In a century and a half, it was never called "the sanctuary," but always "the meeting house."

While at Oberlin, I experienced a confusion of emotion. Although not officially on staff, I preached frequently and began to find that writing sermons was therapy for my spirit and a gift to my soul. Sermon preparation for me would include scanning a host of periodicals, rereading favorite books from seminary classes, and reviewing beloved poems and literature. I would let all these tumble around in my head for a few days along with passages of scripture and my own life stories, and finally I'd sit down and try to weave everything together into a reflection that I hoped would resonate with others. The response was generally enthusiastic, and this caused me both pleasure and frustration.

Doug and I had never agreed that a copastorate would work for us. There was an associate minister already on staff at First Church and no plans to hire any other pastoral leadership. Since a paid position at First Church was not an option, I had applied for a couple of openings with the national UCC offices in Cleveland, as well as a position with a local community foundation. I was frustrated by coming in second each time and ended up working several part-time jobs of short duration: interim pastorates at small churches in neighboring towns, coordinating student activities for the Oberlin College Environmental Studies Department, and being development director for a grassroots community organizing agency in Lorain, a blue collar steel town a half hour away from Oberlin. These were all good experiences, but not the ideal job in which I would fully discover meaningful ministry. I began to wonder if I would ever find this elusive, "perfect" match.

I experienced clinical depression for the first time in my life, which contributed to my feelings of self-doubt and frustration. The gray winter days of Ohio made me long for family and friends in the South. So, after five years in Oberlin, I persuaded Doug to leave First Church and follow me back to North Carolina. We spent a miserable year in Black Mountain where I had been offered an administrative post at a local community college before finally landing in Raleigh in 1997. Doug had received approval and funds to initiate a "new church start," and I had accepted the position of executive director at Safe Space, a domestic violence program serving several rural counties just north of Raleigh. We bought a house that backed up to the buffer zone surrounding Falls Lake, a short walk through the woods from our back yard. Once again, I experienced the joy of swimming out from shore on warm summer evenings and letting the tensions of the day slip away. This was indeed water for a thirsty part of my soul, and I was grateful to be back in a place that felt like home.

Let the floods clap their hands;
let the hills sing together for joy.

PSALM 98:8

Helping to birth a new congregation is a hard task. We had many questions. How do we establish an identity? Where can we meet? Who will provide music? Who will help with child care? In the end, we blitzed two zip code areas with a pamphlet, "Are You Looking for a Progressive Church?" and a postcard featuring the backs of three naked babies, "When It Comes to Teaching Tolerance, Have You Ever Felt That the Church Was More Than a Little Behind?" Although some recipients felt they had received irreverent or even scandalous solicitations (we had some nasty messages on our answer machine accusing us of child pornography), others felt that this might be the kind of faith community they were looking for. On the first Sunday of North Raleigh United Church's existence, Palm Sunday, over 120 people gathered in the auditorium of Durant Middle School. A choir from the Congolese congregation meeting at our sister church, Community U.C.C., gifted us with their witness and song. I preached the very next week, Easter Sunday, on hope.

In North Raleigh United's infancy, I found real joy in helping to shape an intentional community of people drawn together by a shared view of what it means to be church. No sharp theological divides, here. Those who found the church knew that this new congregation was unabashedly liberal and openly inclusive of all persons. From the start, process became as important as outcome in decision making. Relationship was valued over results. When our declaration as an Open and Affirming congregation caused North Raleigh to be denied standing at the Eastern North Carolina Association meeting in 1999, this community of faith had an inner strength to move forward in spite of the pain, anger, and feelings of isolation. Just last year, in October of 2003, North Raleigh successfully ended a long struggle for acceptance and was granted standing in the Association.

North Raleigh United meets near the point where the Neuse River emerges from Falls Lake. This confluence of waters has shaped North Raleigh's view of sacred ecology. Each year, several families spend a day in kayaks picking up trash along the river. The youth group built a bird-viewing stand at the shore of the lake. Spring camping retreats find families tenting side by side at Beaverdam Park, and Easter sunrise services are celebrated on top of the dam. It has been a joy to be part of a worshiping community that sees the important connection between Earth and faith. Like Matthew Fox, I am glad to be singing hymns on Sunday mornings that celebrate creation and original blessing rather than shame and "original" sin.

My position with Safe Space was rewarding but exhausting. A new agency, only two years old when I arrived, Safe Space was experiencing natural growing pains. I found myself establishing administrative policies and procedures, hiring (and firing) staff, writing grant proposals, raising funds for the purchase and renovation of a large Victorian house for a shelter, and handling emergency calls from clients and staff. I had never before been in a position of directing an agency or supervising staff, and now I had to oversee a large budget, deal with security and risk issues unique to an organization that is in contact with violent offenders as a matter of course, and mediate staff conflict. I wore a pager almost every day. It was incredibly stressful. The rewards, however, were seeing the dedication of a beautiful new shelter and hearing formerly abused women speak their gratitude for accompanying them into a new life. I saw that working in the nonprofit arena was a form of ministry that called on every ounce of my resourcefulness and administrative and people skills. However, the combination of starting a new congregation and directing Safe Space was too much, and I decided to look for nonprofit opportunities that were less stressful.

Since August of 2000, I have been the executive director of North Carolina Legal Education Assistance Foundation (NC LEAF), a statewide loan-repayment-assistance program for law school graduates choosing public interest careers. The young attorneys who received help from NC LEAF to pay back their law school loans were actively helping the state's poorest citizens have equal access to justice. I was promoting this effort by helping them stay in the careers they love. Also, since my position at NC LEAF was only three-quarters time, I was able to persuade George Reed, executive director of the North Carolina Council of Churches, to hire me for an additional fifteen hours a week as a program associate.

Working at the North Carolina Council of Churches allows me to feed the activist part of my soul. My earlier passion for building bridges between cultures continues to fuel my work with antiracism initiatives, Latino advocacy, and an oral history project with the Lumbee tribe in the southeastern part of the state. I am energized and inspired by my colleagues at the council, as well as by the people I meet all over North Carolina who are working ecumenically for the common good. By combining my roles at NC LEAF and the North Carolina Council of Churches with my ongoing volunteer leadership at North Raleigh United, I have found a mostly happy balance. Perhaps, sometime in the future, I will find one position that offers activism, spiritual reflection, and leadership, and the satisfaction of helping those in need one person at a time. But, for now, I find this curious blending of priestly and prophetic to be the right ministry for me.

The past few years have been a time of deepening spiritual awareness in which I have found wise women teachers and companions. As a board member of the Triangle Interfaith Alliance, I have developed dear friendships with women who are devout Muslims, Buddhists, Jews, and Sikhs. I have chanted with one friend in front of her family altar and sat cross-legged on the floor next to another at her mosque, a veil over my head. I have prayed with my spiritual companion, a woman rabbi, and eaten a communal meal with a Sikh friend after worship at her *gurud-wara*, or temple. These connections strengthen my sense of the divine feminine as I soak up new expressions of spirit and delight in the God(dess)-light I see in the faces of these strong, good women.

My life has also been deeply touched by knowing Sister Evelyn Mattern, a colleague at the North Carolina Council of Churches, who died recently, and too soon, of cancer. She was a poet, activist, and shining example of how to live an authentic spiritual life. Alas for Albert Schweitzer, he has been replaced!

Another strong Catholic woman and former nun, Gail Phares, has shown me the true measure of courage and persistence in witnessing and resisting injustice. She encouraged me to go with her on a Witness for Peace delegation to Colombia last year, much to the consternation of my family and friends. I made the decision to go on this trip after taking stock of the very real danger involved. I became aware of an inner conviction that I was not going to let fear keep me from standing with those who experience oppression and violence. As I reflect on this, it seems a natural continuation of my advocacy for abused women at Safe Space, as well as an outgrowth of my solidarity with the people of Latin America, which began in Mexico.

To me, Colombia was a land of guns and orchids. I looked into the eyes of people who knew they faced death every day and yet were able to sing and grow gardens.

> Let the sea roar, and all that fills it;
> the world and those who live in it.
>
> PSALM 98:7

The past few years have provided opportunities for my watery nature to reconnect with the life-giving rivers and ocean of North Carolina, the state of my birth. Long summer afternoons spent floating down a river on a kayak or swimming in Falls Lake, just a walk through the woods from our house, have blessed me with solace and, as Wendell Berry says, "the peace of wild things."

Not long ago, I found myself alone on an empty expanse of beach watching the waves wash shells upon the shore. I remembered Anne Morrow Lindbergh's book, *Gift from the Sea,* which I had read over twenty years before when I first embarked on marriage, family, and career. I thought of how much water had passed through my life since that time, of how many shells and fragments of shells had tumbled together and created the multihued mosaic that is now my life.

I realized that my path of ministry has never been a traditional one. I cannot describe it in terms of a "call." Rather, I have found that my experiences of activism, reflection, and secular and religious work have been pieced together into an unfinished kaleidoscope of colors, which continues to grow. The pattern is beautiful, but I am too close to see it completely. I look forward to more surprises. I find that I need fewer answers and more questions, that I am content to live in what Gilda Radner called "the delicious ambiguity" that is life.

I walked along through the waves, then stopped and scooped up a pile of shells, letting them slide through my fingers. Sun glinted from their edges. The incoming tide roared and swirled around my ankles. God still comes to me in the form of many waters.

# THE ROAD TO EMMAUS (AND SIBUNDOY)

**North Raleigh United Church, February 2, 2003**

※

## DENISE CUMBEE LONG

**SCRIPTURES: Psalm 146; Luke 24:13–32**

Like all good theology, this sermon must be told as a story. It is not only a story about me but also a tale about people I have encountered in the last two weeks whose lives are very different from mine. I have looked in their eyes and seen God. And I have walked with them a short way along a road I never thought to travel. I have been cursed with the knowledge of their pain. And, I have been blessed by their courage to live and love.

The story begins with my decision to go on a ten-day trip to Colombia as part of a twenty-seven-member delegation sponsored by Witness for Peace. The purpose of this delegation was to speak with people in Colombia who have been directly impacted by our U.S. foreign policy, now in its third year, called "Plan Colombia." Few people know that Colombia receives from the United States the third largest amount of military assistance of any country with only Israel and Egypt getting more foreign military aid. Few also know that our tax dollars go to fund a war plan that has been pitched to the public as a counternarcotic and counterinsurgency strategy but that, in reality, is more like throwing gasoline on a fire.

The United States is heavily funding both Colombian security forces and counternarcotic efforts that involve aerial fumigation of drug crops. Both of these policies have escalated an already devastating war and have worsened the refugee and public health crises. The Colombian military is known as among the most abusive in the hemisphere. They have also been directly linked to terrorist paramilitary organizations. The aerial eradication program involves using U.S.-made planes and helicopters to seek out illegal drug growers and spray their coca crops. What has happened, however, is that toxic chemicals are repeatedly sprayed on rural Colombian communities and fragile Amazonian rain forest.

The cost of this program has been almost two billion dollars. Has it reduced drug supply? The U.S. government's own statistics show that drug cultivation in Colombia increased 25 percent in the last year. Has funding the Colombian military curbed violence? According to Human Rights Watch, since Plan Colombia began in 2000, civilian deaths have increased from twelve to twenty per day. Although both the leftist guerrilla group, known as the FARC, and the right-wing paramilitary groups use narco trafficking to fund their dirty war, U.S. policy seems to have particularly strengthened the brutal right-wing paramilitaries. These groups regularly kill and threaten Colombian civilians and have grown by over 500 percent since 1996.

Witness for Peace delegations to Colombia have the purpose of engaging ordinary U.S. citizens in witnessing and challenging unjust U.S. economic and military policies. This happens by giving people like me an opportunity to listen to people like displaced campesino farmers, Afro-Colombian refugees who were forced off their land, indigenous leaders of dwindling tribes, outspoken priests, and courageous union organizers. And when people like me listen to the stories of these

Colombians, we come back home changed. That's the magic. It's as if we had been walking a road with a stranger and suddenly knew that our hearts were burning within us.

Our delegation first flew to Miami for a two-day orientation. Part of this process was to make sure that we really knew what we were getting into and that we really understood the risks involved. We had briefings on Colombian history and politics and lots of role plays involving "what if" scenarios. What should we do if the bus is stopped at a roadblock by the FARC or the paramilitaries? What should we have in our emergency packs in case we were kidnapped? What should we say and not say in public places?

It was a pretty grueling and sobering two days, and it gave us all time to reflect on whether this was really what we felt called to do right now. In the end, everyone decided to go, and we flew to Bogotá for three days of meetings with environmental activists, labor organizers, human rights workers, and policy experts. Security protocol was strict. We could never go anywhere alone. Curfew was ten at night, and we had to have our emergency packs with us at all times. We also had to count off in pairs anytime we walked or traveled anywhere in order to make sure everyone was accounted for. This became such a habit, that even as we walked through the Miami airport on our trip home, we started calling out "A1, A2, B1, B2!" just for old times' sake!

And what a motley crew we were! There was our delegation leader, Gail Phares, a former nun and cofounder of Witness for Peace, whom I have known for twenty years, and Kia, an organic farmer from Snow Camp, North Carolina. There was Lynette, a Puerto Rican physician from San Francisco who runs a clinic for homeless people, and her partner, Sandra, a native Colombian from Medellin, who now heads up Global Exchange in California. There was Joseph Jordan, the Chair of African American Studies at UNC-Chapel Hill, and Megan, an alternative fuel specialist from Maine. There were Kate, John, and Mansur, longtime activists on Latin American issues, and Danette, a union organizer. There were several idealistic college students who spoke terrific Spanish, a journalist whose wife cofounded *USA Today,* and a radio broadcaster who took his recording equipment along so he could do a series of programs that will be aired later this year at over 150 stations nationwide. Add a former Sandinista from Nicaragua, a chaplain from a Kentucky college, a legislative aid to a North Carolina congressman, an immigration attorney (married to the Nicaraguan Sandinista) and an eighty-year-old nun who loved a night out at a Bogotá bar, and you'll have just a taste of what a diverse crew we were.

We stayed together as one large group for the initial time in Bogotá. One day we traveled by bus to the squatter settlements on the outskirts of the city. We had been invited by a community of displaced Afro-Colombians to visit their homes in the sprawling refugee area known as Soacha. Afro-Colombians, whose ancestors were brought to the country as slaves by the Spaniards centuries ago, make up about a third of the population of Colombia and formerly occupied much of the Pacific coast. Now, their rich, forested lands have become the target for armed groups seeking emeralds, gold, and oil. They, like two million others of Colombia's most vulnerable citizens, are internal refugees, "the displaced ones," as they are called.

The Afro-Colombian leaders in Soacha invited us to walk their dusty roads with them, see their homes where there is water only once a week, and hear their stories of pain. They spoke of losing a beautiful land they loved, of having family members threatened or killed, of experiencing racism and exploitation. They cried when they spoke to us. We cried with them.

But they also spoke of hope, of building a school, of organizing for change, and of someday returning to their homes by the sea. They cooked for us, broke bread with us, and we danced together in a hot cinder-block building to the percussive sounds of salsa, rumba, and *cumbia*.

After a few days in Bogotá, our group split in half, with one delegation traveling to Medellín and the other going south to the *departamiento*, or state, of Putumayo. This was my group. Previous delegations to Colombia had visited Putumayo in order to see the devastating effects of the aerial spraying near the border of Ecuador. Our group, however, had been invited to a small town in the northern section of the region by some outspoken priests. Sibundoy is a picturesque village of flowers, stuccoed houses, and mountains. The name *Sibundoy*, comes from an indigenous word meaning "Door of the Sun." Located at a higher altitude than lower Putumayo, its climate is too cool for coca crops, and it had largely escaped the violence experienced by other towns in the Amazon area. At least, until a couple of months ago.

In November, the FARC guerrillas kidnapped the daughter of the mayor of a neighboring town. In response, a military unit from the Colombian 24th Brigade was dispatched and set up operations near Sibundoy. Shortly afterward, the paramilitary groups began to appear, and the killings began. First one group would sweep through, identify people who supposedly were not on their side, and either force them from their homes, kidnap, or kill them. Then the opposing group would do the same. The military and police would do nothing. And, as we heard from so many families, it was impossible to be seen as neutral. The armed groups would demand allegiance. Not helping them meant helping the "enemy."

When we arrived on January 21, there had been twenty-six killings since the end of November. The paramilitaries had swept through the night before we arrived, forcing twenty-five families from their homes and spraying graffiti on houses. Seven local priests seized on the idea of hosting a mass for peace at the church on the town square. They begged us to come. The idea was that an international presence that was visible and publicized would be a good thing. Our little delegation of blue-shirted gringos might make the armed groups realize that their actions were not going unnoticed, and that the international community cared about what was happening.

When we arrived, we were met at the tiny airport, an hour from Sibundoy, by Padre Raoul, the priest at a small town bordering Sibundoy, and a church worker named Marta. We boarded a bus for the hour drive. I sat with Marta and listened to her speak of the families she knew affected by the recent violence. "The police do not protect us!" she said. "They let the paramilitaries do whatever they want. Everyone in the village knows who the paramilitaries are. But the police claim they do not know." I listened with a heavy heart. She was a young, vibrant woman of about thirty, and she knew too much. But then, we looked out the window, and she pointed out some of the exotic flowers as we drove past. She told me that almost every day she goes into the forest to collect orchids. She tries to save and grow some of the rarer species, which are slowly disappearing. This, she says, gives life to her soul. This is her way of defying the forces of violence and death. It is an act of spiritual resistance.

Padre Raoul had the bus stop at his church on the way in to Sibundoy. He showed us a poster of a pregnant woman addressing a group of men with guns, asking them to use negotiations rather than violence to seek the change they want. "This," he said sadly, "is a controversial poster. It is legal. It is peaceful. But, I have been threatened because I put it up in the church."

But, Padre Raoul, like Marta, was also a man who did not let fear and sadness overwhelm him. He loved to laugh, he loved a good joke (he had several about priests), and he thought it was very funny when we told him that our code phrase for danger, or for letting someone in our group know they were saying something they shouldn't, was "It's snowing in Chicago." He didn't know English, but he repeated that phrase over and over again, laughing all the time.

After lunch, we met with some of the members of two indigenous groups in the area, the Cametsan and the Inga. They were dressed with striped ponchos, brilliantly colored shawls, and strands and strands of colorful seed beads. They spoke a language that less than three thousand people in the world still knew. They told us of being forced to leave their ancestral lands by the armed groups moving into the area, of being threatened, of feeling abandoned. They spoke of their fear—fear of losing their culture, their lands, and their children. They told us they were afraid there would come a day when no one would be left who could speak their tongue. Padre Raoul and his friend, Padre Campo, sat on the bench at the back of the room and cried.

One indigenous woman finished her tearful story and thanked us for coming to be with them. She said that we all had the same mother, our Mother Earth, who gives us life, no matter which race we are, and she invited us to give reverence to that Mother by touching the ground. Silently, she leaned forward and touched the floor. Silently, every person in the room bent to touch the ground, and white hands mingled with brown ones. It was a sacred moment as the light began to fade in Sibundoy, the Door of the Sun.

That night we met with the seven priests of the Sibundoy valley and the bishop of the entire state of Putumayo. They told us of the effects the aerial spraying were having farther south, of entire communities losing all the crops they had, of hunger, of sick children with skin rashes and diarrhea. They looked us in the eyes and asked us to ask our government to stop this toxic destruction. They spoke of how often they hear the stories of families who have lost members to violence or displacement. Their eyes were filled with pain for people they served. And yet, they took out guitars at the end of the meeting and sang into the evening. As we walked back across the deserted square to our hotel, we realized that no one was out. A lone horse wandered along the empty street but all other signs of life were gone. Windows and doors were shut tightly against the night. Fear was palpable.

The next morning, we got ready for the peace mass. A group of about fifty displaced campesino families met us with white flags and walked with us down the street to the church. The priests had told us that they didn't expect many to attend, maybe one hundred. It was a weekday morning when most people were working in the fields or at their businesses, and besides they had only decided to do it the week before. But, as we walked, we noticed more and more people going in the same direction, and when we reached the church, it was standing room only. Over a thousand people were there!

The church was cool, with pink marble walls and statues of the Virgin holding a baby. The bishop and priests were resplendent in their white robes and colorful stoles, and above their heads someone had made a silvery wire banner that read, "Sembramos La Paz," "We Sow Peace." Sunlight dropped like a blessing through the windows.

It was a powerful event. The bishop spoke forcefully against violence. The mayor welcomed our group and thanked us for our solidarity. The *taita*, or elder of the Cametsan people, spoke eloquently of being united in a struggle for justice. Three of our delegation made us proud by speaking from the heart about our desire to stand with the Colombian people, to listen to them, and then to go home and work hard for changes on their behalf.

Children ran back and forth up the steps to the altar. A couple of small dogs trotted around the aisles. The music was miked from a soloist and a keyboardist who chose some controversial songs about peace, faith, and the struggle for justice. Our friend, Padre Campo, the main organizer of the service, and one of the most outspoken priests, gave a fiery homily. He is a short, wiry man with dark black hair. "Our God is a God of Life," he said. "We defy the forces which work against it." His eyes flashed as he looked out at the sea of faces in front of him. "We will not let violence and fear destroy us. We know there are members of armed groups in our town. We know you are out there. We know you can hear us. Listen to us now! We are united. Stop the killing! Join us in working for peace." His words were broadcast over the radio to the whole valley of Sibundoy.

The priests and the bishop began the liturgy for the eucharist. I caught some of the familiar words, only in Spanish, as the call and response echoed back and forth through the church from the leaders and the congregation. "Lift up your hearts." "We lift up our hearts...." "On the night he was betrayed...." "And in the same manner, he took the cup, saying. 'This is my blood, poured out for you.'" The rise and fall of a thousand voices swelled around me.

As the priests lifted up the chalice, I thought of Oscar Romero in El Salvador, shot down while performing the mass. I thought of Padre Acide, a friend and mentor of these priests, who had been killed in the same way five years ago not far from Sibundoy, assassinated while saying mass. His crime had been speaking out against drug trafficking and helping the people grow alternative food crops. I saw the priests in front of me, bravely standing before the crowd, and I realized that this eucharist, this communion, was also an act of spiritual resistance.

The people came forward to receive the mass—old, young, campesino, store owner, indigenous grandmother, government official. We stood shoulder to shoulder, and the wafer was sweet on our tongues. When the service ended, our group was engulfed by people who wanted to welcome us. We were hugged, we were touched, and we were embraced by a hundred hands. "Thank you for coming here!" we heard over and over.

But as I was speaking with a group of tiny indigenous women, I was tapped on the shoulder. It was our delegation leader who said, "It's snowing in Chicago. Go to the back of the church and stand with the group. Go as quickly as you can."

Apparently, Padre Raoul, who had joked with us at lunch yesterday, had been approached by our friend Marta. She had seen men on the steps of the church who were known to be with the paramilitaries. When she told this to Padre Raoul, he quickly used our code phrase to let Gail and others in our group know that we could be in danger. We used a cell phone to call our bus driver, and he drove the bus right up to the steps of the church. People still milled around us, innocently offering us their well wishes. An old woman gave us apples.

We stood tightly together by twos and then walked out into the bright sunshine. As we stepped to the bus, I thought of how vulnerable we were at that moment. I had a brief taste of what fear is like, of what it must be like to live like this all the time—a target of violence. I thought of the people I had embraced, of the priests who had spoken. I was leaving; they were not.

On our final morning in Putumayo, we held morning reflections in the courtyard of the church in Mocoa where Padre Campo directed his pastoral services work. Each morning we were there, some of the priests had joined us for a devotional time. One from our group would begin, and then one of the priests would end. On our final morning, Greg, one of the younger members of our group who works with a Latino agency in Rhode Island, asked us to find a partner. I was sitting next to Padre Campo, so he and I turned to each other.

Greg asked us to look into the eyes of our partner, to think about what that person's life must be like, to remember when we first saw that person laugh, and when we saw him or her cry. I looked into dark brown eyes filled with kindness and pain. I saw unspeakable sadness. I saw a deep, deep compassion. And I saw courage of a kind I had never seen before. This man knew he could die any day. But his love was stronger than his fear.

My eyes filled with tears. His did too. He whispered, "Tu me tocas mucho (You touch me deeply)." The tears spilled down my cheeks. Padre Campo reached into his pocket, took out a neatly folded handkerchief, and gently wiped my tears. I could not stop weeping.

After we finished a short time of silence, Padre Campo's friend, Fernand, read the scripture that the priest had selected for that morning. It was the passage about the two friends walking the road to Emmaus. "This is one of my favorite passages," Campo said. "It speaks to us with hope. The road to Emmaus is one of sadness. We think there is only death and despair."

I was reminded of what Frederick Buechner had written about this same story:

> [Emmaus is] the place we go in order to escape…. Emmaus is whatever we do or wherever we go to make ourselves forget that the world holds nothing sacred: that even the wisest and bravest and loveliest decay and die; that even the noblest ideas that men have had—ideas about love and freedom and justice—have always in time been twisted out of shape.[i]

"But," Padre Campo said, "Christ comes to us on this road of sadness, as he always does. Christ is our traveling companion. The one who walks with us, shares our bread, and gives us hope. Our souls are resurrected over and over again, and death does not have the final say."

Campo Elias De la Cruz. Your first name, "Campo," means "field, or land." You have committed yourself to serving the poor who scrape their existence from the land and to those who have been displaced from land they love. Your second name, "Elias," means "Elijah." You are a prophet. You speak truth even though it may kill you. And your last name, "De la Cruz" means "Of the Cross." You are the risen Christ, the voice of life and hope to many who still walk the dusty roads of sadness in Sibundoy. I have looked into your eyes, and I have seen God.

Padre Campo Elias De la Cruz. May you be kept safe. May the people of Sibundoy feel that their hearts were warmed because of your love. May the brief accompaniment of our delegation bring you some sense of support and strength on your own Emmaus road. And may we all travel together toward a world of peace and justice.

i. *The Magnificent Defeat*, (New York: Seabury Press, 1966), pp. 85–86.

# BLESSINGS ON THE JOURNEY

ANN H. McLAUGHLIN

Creation is continuous and never stops. And neither do blessing and blessings. Blessing is the word behind the word, the desire behind the creation. For God the Creator, like any artist, is not indifferent or neutral to his/her work of art. Like any parent, God loves her creation and that love which is an unconditional sending forth into existence is blessing....

Blessing involves relationship: one does not bless without investing something of oneself into the receiver of one's blessing. And one does not receive blessing oblivious of its gracious giver. A blessing spirituality is a relating spirituality. And if it is true that all of creation flows from a single, loving source, then all of creation is blessed and is a blessing, atom to atom, molecule to molecule, organism to organism, land to plants, plants to animals, animals to other animals, people to people, and back to atoms, molecules, plants, fishes. On and on *Dabhar* [the energetic creative word of God] flows, on and on blessing flows. For where there is *Dabhar*, there is blessing.[1]

MATTHEW FOX

As I begin writing this, I am in the third month of my retirement from the ministry of pastoral counseling. As I look back over life in relation to the church, I am almost overwhelmed by the sheer volume of information and experience. So my task is to try to decide on what is most important in telling my story. I experience myself as basically a fairly low energy, artistic, poetic, mystical, introverted person. As is true of all of us, life has presented me with conflicts. The Chinese characters for "crisis," which combines the symbols of "danger" and "opportunity," hold great meaning for me. I experience my daily life as a constant progression of crises, both large and small, that invite me to make decisions that empower me to be a cocreator with God.

The thought that I might be a cocreator with God actually came upon me when I was in my twenties and in seminary, reading Paul Tillich. Up until that time I had for the most part focused myself spiritually and intellectually on "following the rules" that I had incorporated into my soul during my childhood, at home, church, and school. But I am getting ahead of my story.

When I observe the events of life as danger and opportunity, I attempt to find the quiet place, the transition, the space between the danger and the opportunity. This is the space of prayer, meditation, discernment, that will allow the decision to emerge. This process that I can identify and articulate at this point in my life has not always been so clear to me, but rather it has been a lifetime journey that I hope has still yet a ways to go.

I was born in 1935 in the Great Depression. My twenty-year-old mother had been raised as a Presbyterian with strict, often harsh, perfectionistic high standards. My twenty-six-year-old dad had been raised in a fairly pietistic manner. He was the son of a Methodist father and a Baptist mother. A story about my dad's family, which only much later puzzled me, was that when he was a young boy on the farm, his father would hitch up two buggies on Sunday mornings, and his mother would drive half of the eight children to the Baptist Church, and his father would drive the other four children to the Methodist Church. My mother sometimes referred to her mother-in-law as a "hard-shelled" Baptist, and although I never got a direct definition of that term from her, the connotation in the tone of her voice was quite clear. Mother didn't like my paternal grandmother.

Mother had been raised by her mother's aunt who became my grandmother's housekeeper when my paternal grandfather died in the influenza epidemic of 1918, leaving a thirty-three-year-old widow with three children all under five years of age. My grandmother went back to work as a legal secretary and worked continuously until she died of cancer at age sixty-seven. Aunt Maggie, my grandmother's aunt, had never married and had supported herself as a supervisor of the cleaning staff at a local hotel until she took the position as my grandmother's housekeeper. She could be described as a Victorian spinster who had never married, at least partly because her father chased away the only man who wanted to marry her. Aunt Maggie was a constant presence in my home when I was growing up, although she had in fact left this life about eight years before my birth. I experienced her (through my mother) as prim, proper, starched, fastidious, hardworking, and joyless.

My parents moved in with my paternal grandmother when they got married. Mother worked in the office of my dad's brother-in-law's hardware company. Daddy was clerking in a law firm while he waited to pass the bar exam. His father had died of a heart attack in his early sixties, leaving my grandmother a lost soul who never really found herself again. By the time of my birth, sixteen months after they were married, Daddy was using alcohol to excess to mask his depression and anxiety. Mother, of course, had resigned her job as soon as her pregnancy had begun to "show." They continued to live with my grandmother until I was two years old, at which time they moved about a mile and a half away into a house that they had built, going into a debt that was somewhat frightening.

Times were hard in those years. The extended family helped each other in many ways. They loaned or gave each other money for the bare necessities and for educational expenses; older ones who were more established shepherded the younger ones, and younger ones at times moved back in with a parent or an older sibling. I have the sense that my dad did the best he could and didn't count the cost of helping his family, friends, or clients, and my mother, now over sixty years later, can remember debts not repaid. She has always been the bookkeeper, and he was the salesman.

I grew up in Greensboro, North Carolina, then a town of about fifty thousand people. It was large enough to have several colleges, both black and white, and to support occasional cultural entertainment, in particular musical concerts. It was small enough to provide a real sense of community in the neighborhood, school, and church. The community plus an extended family of eventually twenty-one cousins and eighteen aunts and uncles offered to me a sense of security that was often absent in the anxiety and depression at home.

I was a tomboy. In my immediate neighborhood, which I was allowed to roam before I went to school, there were no girls. I played hide and seek, kick the can, bicycle tag, cops and robbers, cowboys and Indians, kick ball, rollerbat, and other games that boys organize. We were on the last street in the city limits, and behind us were woods, fields, and creeks. We explored all of them, and my love of nature developed because when we were exploring, there were no parents around to remind me to act like a girl.

When Pearl Harbor was bombed in December 1941, I was in the first grade. As the country mobilized for war, the family, neighborhood, school, and church seemed to be interlocking pieces of the structure of society that supported each other. The American flag was displayed in some churches, and many school classrooms opened each morning with a devotional time that included prayer, a Bible reading, and the Pledge of Allegiance.

Several years ago a few of my high school friends, who incidentally had been together for all twelve years of public school, gathered for lunch, and we affirmed unanimously that we had had a very special childhood, living in a community where we were known and had felt safe. We had a simple way of life where the rules were mostly clear and explicit. Of course, there were some people who broke the rules, like the cheerleader who got pregnant or the rich young man who totaled his father's car as he exceeded the speed limit by about thirty miles an hour. But the churches and schools demonstrated a Christian faith and ethic that seemed to fit neatly with the democracy that was emphasized and taught in the schools. With the ever-present threat of World War II, my perception of the world was that we democratic Christians were the bearers of the torch of freedom against the Axis who had no regard for either democracy or Christianity.

Again, the lines and the rules were clear. I had two uncles and a cousin who served in the Armed Forces, the cousin dying in Europe— I never knew where, nor did the family. I never really knew him because he was the oldest cousin, thirteen years older than I, and lived in Raleigh, seventy-five miles away. But when my uncle told my dad, that was one of the few times that I ever saw him cry.

On the home front, everyone recycled metal, rubber, tin cans, cooking fat, paper; and we bought many necessities including sugar, shoes, tires, and gasoline with rationing stamps in addition to money. When we went to the beach, we had to put blankets over the windows at night so as not to silhouette American transport ships against the lights because German submarines lurked off the coast to destroy men and materials that were being sent to aid our allies in Europe.

When the war ended in 1945, the rationing stamps were thrown away and the recycling was largely ignored, except that my family continued to recycle newspapers until that practice began to come back into favor in the sixties. By then saving had become so much a part of my character that I have continued to recycle and reuse as we did during the Depression and the War.

The next year my dad joined Alcoholics Anonymous and was struggling with his serious addiction. I was very proud and relieved that he was making a very determined effort. After twenty years of drinking to excess, it was hard for him, and he had a number of "slips" back into the alcohol. Nonetheless, we began to have a few more dollars to spend on, if not luxuries, at least more than the necessities. I began to know my dad in a more relaxed and trusting way. When he wasn't drinking, he was funny, fun, generous, charming, and adventurous. I liked to be with him, to go places with him, to listen to the baseball games on the radio with him. Television was just becoming available, and we didn't have one. I liked to talk with him about the law (he was an attorney), politics, religion, and life in general.

When I was fifteen, my dad died of a heart attack. It was sudden and completely unexpected. I came home from a band trip to find him gone. Life changed. The house was paid for, and there was some insurance, but basically, we lived on my mother's salary. We were back into sparse times again. My brother who was thirteen took a job in a restaurant after school, and I saw less of him. I missed my dad terribly, but no one talked about grief in those days. We soldiered on.

The excitement I might have felt in high school was always clouded by my sense of loss. I did well academically and finished second in my class, played in the band, took piano lessons, but didn't practice much. I had a few boyfriends, appreciated my close group of girlfriends, and was fairly active in the Methodist Youth Fellowship. I grew close to a young woman, a college student who was the adviser to youth. She was majoring in religious education at Greensboro College, and I think that was when I began to be attracted to ministry as a vocation.

I graduated from high school, and with scholarships and rather meager savings, my mother helped me scrape together the money for four years at Duke University. There was never any thought that I wouldn't graduate or that I would take more than four years to do it. The sacrifices had been too great to waste any time with this opportunity. At Duke I was thrust into a much more challenging world of ideas and customs. It seemed to me that a lot of the other young women were huge (several over six feet tall), aggressive, fast talking, and Yankees. Quite a shock for an introverted, provincial southern girl! I plunged into completing the required courses and began to explore the alternatives for a major: education, sociology, psychology, religion. The influences of the church and schools, both of which had nurtured me though my early years were the top contenders. I was fascinated by the knowledge and faith of my professors, and made the decision to major in religion and become a Christian education director in the church.

I met a young man from Virginia—introverted, serious, and interested in getting a Ph.D. in chemistry and teaching at the college level. He was a member of the Evangelical and Reformed Church. He had applied for a Danforth Fellowship, which would pay all his expenses for his degree. I was offered a tuition scholarship to Chicago Theological Seminary (CTS), a UCC seminary. He applied to the University of Chicago, and was accepted. We were married two weeks after we graduated from Duke, and we were on our way. It seemed to me that everything had fallen into our laps. On a warm spring day in our last weeks at Duke, I met a woman campus minister, and I told her that I was going to attend CTS and work on a degree in Christian education. She said, "You don't want to stop with the master's degree; you should get a divinity degree and get ordained." I think that was the first time that I had ever entertained that thought.

Chicago was another challenge—higher academic standards, overwhelming amounts of reading and writing, an abrupt midwestern urban culture, cold blustery winters, and dirt and pollution. I was often depressed and homesick. The winter seemed unending. Yet I kept going, thanks to the exciting ideas, the great minds of my professors and the writings they assigned, the more liberal approach to faith and society, and the fellowship of the students. Chicago Theological

Seminary was an intentional Christian community such as I had never experienced before. The classrooms, chapel, single student housing, and married student housing were all within walking distance. My husband and I chose to live in the seminary's married student housing rather than the university housing, and it was a fortuitous choice.

At the seminary, women were well under 10 percent of the class and probably nearer to 5 percent. I remember only one other married woman who was a student. Many times I was asked, "Why did you decide to come to seminary?" And the tone of voice was different from what I experienced when a man was asked that question. I took secret pleasure in feeling myself something of a pioneer. I had always been fascinated by those early women who had the courage to leave their home communities and go off to a far country. However, I expected to tough out the four years in the far country and then return home to the South.

In 1963, we came back home to North Carolina, now a family of four, with a two-year-old daughter and a ten-month-old son. We joined the United Church of Christ in Chapel Hill and began the reentry into "normal" family life, after having been students for the past twenty years. The United Church of Christ was a church home that felt comfortable to both of us. Neither my husband nor I had finished our degrees. He needed to complete his Ph.D. dissertation in chemistry, and I needed to finish my master's thesis in religion and personality. We bought a little house with help from our respective parents, and we spent our "spare time" working on the papers. It was hard work with two little kids.

Eventually the papers got written, and we soldiered on with our responsibilities as a young family, but the marriage became increasingly difficult. Having put so much energy into academics, we had neglected to learn how to make the necessary changes that a relationship requires to remain viable. I worked for two years in a half-time position as a youth minister in a Presbyterian church, and my husband worked in a post-doctoral position at the University of North Carolina. Then it all fell apart. We visited a marriage counselor, who referred us to separate psychotherapists, but marriage counseling was not a very well-developed discipline at that time, and we were not able to repair the rents in our relationship. So we agreed to a divorce with joint custody for the children.

When my job as youth minister came to an end, I began work in the Chapel Hill Day Center, which was housed in the United Church of

Christ. I stayed there for three years, then went to summer school and took classes to develop secretarial and bookkeeping skills. I then went to work for a real estate development company. It was an important experience because it convinced me that I didn't want to spend my life in business.

Then came a letter from CTS stating that they were involved in a program to encourage people, especially women, who had obtained a master of arts to have their transcripts evaluated to determine how many courses they would need to qualify for a master's of divinity degree and thus be eligible for ordination. I activated that process and was delighted to discover that I needed only three courses to complete the master's of divinity. How could I refuse? Another blessing had fallen softly on my head.

One of the courses that I needed to complete the degree was a clinical course, in which I worked as a minister under supervision. I chose the introductory clinical pastoral education course at Duke and worked as a chaplain, which led to training in pastoral counseling. As I was progressing in the program, I was becoming more convinced that this was a good match for me as a minister. My interests in spirituality, psychology, and education all seemed to come together in my studies; my introversion was not a liability; and in addition, as I was learning to heal the wounds of others, I was finding healing for my own wounds.

A funny thing happened on the way to ordination. Jim Riddle, the pastor at The Community Church of Chapel Hill, an interdenominational church that had formed during the civil rights struggles, was an ordained UCC pastor. I had joined that church after my divorce, and Jim became my mentor to shepherd me through the ordination process. In my ordination paper for the Church and Ministry Commission, I used Paul Tillich as a major theologian. I realized that he was one of the more liberal theologians, but his writings and lectures had been extremely important to me as I struggled with the conflicts of my conservative Methodist background. My greatest fear was that the commission would question me about my divorce. My surprise and shock was that they ignored the divorce and asked me to describe my stance on the virgin birth. I carefully explained my belief that this was an interpretation by the early church to make a case for the fact that Jesus was the Son of God, but it was not a belief that I literally accepted. The rest of the meeting—and it seemed interminable to me—consisted of the more conservative members trying to convince me of the error of my position. When I left the room for them to vote on my suitability for ordination, I was not at all sure that I would be accepted. I was greatly relieved when I returned for their verdict to find that I had passed. This was my first encounter with the conservative strain of the United Church of Christ, and I discovered that theologically they were not very different from the Methodists with whom I had grown up.

By this time, I was deeply engrossed in the chaplaincy and pastoral counseling training, and Jim made arrangements for my ordination into the Eastern North Carolina Association of the United Church of Christ.

Upon completing my counseling training in 1980, I was required to become a member in the American Association of Pastoral Counselors. This meant writing another paper and making another committee appearance. I eventually found a job at the Life Enrichment Center (now Triangle Pastoral Counseling) in Raleigh. I moved to Raleigh and joined the Community United Church of Christ, where Cally Rogers-Witte was the pastor. Cally and I had met when she had worked for a year without pay at the Community Church in Chapel Hill while she was looking for a paying position. I had been chair of the board of trustees. It was good to be with her again and another blessing in my life.

I have remained at Triangle Pastoral Counseling (TPC) for almost twenty-two years. In that time, I have also been a participating member at Community UCC. I have occasionally officiated at weddings, funerals, baptisms, and communion services and have done supply preaching. But my full-time ministry has been counseling. Our ecumenical center considers itself an extension of the ministry of the local churches. We counsel individuals, couples, and families whose situations are either too difficult or too time-consuming for the full-time parish pastor to take on. Again this has been a blessing for me. The Counseling Center has been a place for my own emotional, intellectual, and spiritual growth. I have worked with colleagues who are Methodist, Baptist, Disciples of Christ, Presbyterian, Roman Catholic, and Episcopalian. My clients have included all of the above plus Jews, atheists, agnostics, a Muslim, a Hindu, and members of small rural denominations whose names I can't remember. I have felt free to explore and incorporate into my faith position theological viewpoints and spiritual disciplines from each of these plus Buddhism and Eastern meditation through yoga.

In addition, working at TPC has been a twenty-two year continuation of the regimen that began with my training. The collegial community, individually and collectively, is committed to intellectual, emotional, and spiritual growth in themselves, their clients, and their colleagues. It is particularly exciting and humbling to have worked in an environment in which every staff member shared these values. It was truly a spiritual community, even though we came from many denominational backgrounds. It would be wonderful if the world could adopt the same level of commitment to listening to each other, respecting each other, resolving differences, and living lovingly and peaceably with each other.

I have appreciated having a church family that has allowed me to stretch myself to become more inclusive, more accepting and loving, more politically active, more ecologically responsible. The inclusive policies of the United Church of Christ have felt comfortable for me as I have grown older, for I now have the theological education and life experience to affirm the simple stirrings that I felt as a child, that we human beings are all one people, children of God, no matter what our gender, color, ethnicity, or sexual orientation. I have appreciated the denominational focus on spiritual growth and social justice, which is a more sophisticated expression of the values that I learned in the church and schools during that "greatest generation" of World War II. And I am proud and humbled to be a descendant of the Pilgrim tradition that saw the authority of the community as more important than the ecclesiastical hierarchy.

My theology of conflict resolution as a way to spiritual growth and social justice has been enhanced by my training as a pastoral counselor and as a member of the United Church of Christ. My studies in Eastern meditation have informed me so that I can more easily find the quiet, still, present moment between the danger and the opportunity. I call that decision place responsible justice with loving-kindness. I'm not always satisfied that I make the best possible decision, but I am satisfied that the process is a valid one that can lead to ever-deeper knowledge of myself, my fellow human beings, and God.

God is good. I have been blessed.

---

1. *Original Blessing* (Santa Fe: Bear & Company, 1983), p. 44.

# MINISTERING TO IMMIGRANTS

MARIA PALMER

*(As told to Robin J. Townsley Arcus)*

I was born in 1960 in Lima, Peru. My father was a Polish immigrant. My mother was born in Peru, but her grandfather had immigrated to Peru from the United States. It was after the Civil War when he left Philadelphia because things were so bad. When one of my sons researched our family tree, he thought it was funny that his ancestors actually left North America for South America, looking for a better life.

My parents were professionals and had worked internationally, and so, comparably, my family was well off. I came to the United States not because I was looking for a better life; I came to the United States as a college exchange student. That is when I became involved with the church.

My family was completely secular. When I was very young, I went to a school run by Canadian nuns because my mother wanted me to learn English. Already by second grade, I knew I was going to fight for justice.

I remember that year grabbing the hand of a classmate and taking her to the office because the teacher wouldn't let her get help for her asthma. I have always felt that you have to stand up to the abuse of power. There was a revolution in Peru in 1968, when the military took over, and I remember we were talking about it in elementary school. The teacher said, "Maria Teresa, we need to focus on the lessons. There's not much we can do about it." And I said, "We need to restore democracy!" I was eight. I guess I have always felt like you cannot put up with bullies and allow people to be run over. That has gotten me into some fights. It's something I got from my parents and grandmother, people who try to do what's right. Maybe I'm not doing it in the grand way I thought I might be when I was a child. We each do what we can in our sphere of influence.

I was drawn to the teachings of Jesus when I came to the United States as an exchange student. I came to Jacksonville State University in Alabama for one year and then had my scholarship renewed. A fantastic campus minister in the Baptist Student Union (BSU) influenced me. He helped me see the relevance of the teachings of Jesus to everyday life. Back in Peru, religion was a compulsory subject. Scriptures and dogma were something to be memorized, as were, for example, the differences between venial and mortal sins. Everything was so theoretical. I used to get into big arguments with my religion teachers. I would argue with them and not do very well on my tests. The other students would say, "You could score 100 on your exams," but I wouldn't answer the questions with the answers they wanted, not things I couldn't agree with!

I loved the ceremony and the pomp, the prayers, but I couldn't live that way. At BSU, we were shown how to live faithfully and with integrity.

I met my husband in college. Mike was also involved with the campus ministry. He was from Alabama, from a Southern Baptist family. We were married in 1980, after my second year of school. That summer we volunteered as missionaries and were sent to Yuma, Arizona. We worked in border towns and out in the farms where people were living in trailer homes and migrant camps. The people spoke Spanish and yet we were supposed to teach Bible school with materials in English! We organized the vacation Bible school our own way. The first day we introduced the Bible, the second day the prophets, the third day we celebrated Christmas, the fourth day we studied the Good Samaritan, and the fifth day we had the crucifixion and the resurrection. I believe you could call that a brief overview! We called it our mission vacation Bible school. We worked with kids right along the border. It was a transforming summer.

One day, immigration agents arrived at our Bible school, which we were holding in a park, and they carried off half of our students! I cried about this, for those people, but also because I wasn't any more documented than the children. After I married Mike, it took more than a year for the Immigration and Naturalization Service (INS) to give me a green card. Luckily, they didn't ask me for documents, probably because I was dressed nicely and looked like a teacher. But I was only twenty years old and to me this seemed like a very ugly thing to do.

One of the agents said, "What are you giving these children? Why are they coming?"

I said, "We are teaching them Bible stories, and all about Jesus. We are giving them the road map for their lives." This was the phrase we used with the kids about Jesus' teachings.

The officer said, "What these children really want is a road map of how to get back in the United States."

Ever since then immigration has been a big part of my mission. It breaks my heart to see people pay five hundred dollars for a work permit that buys them the right to come here and do backbreaking labor. I have seen so many things that are counter to Judeo-Christian ethics of the teachings of Jesus. So I have lobbied and organized meetings; I have done many things. At my church, Iglesia Unida de Cristo, one thing we have worked hard on is our covenant. It reads, "Because we have been called to be a community where there are no foreigners, we are united in God's work." We are not going to ask people about their immigration status.

College was such a transforming experience. I finished my degree in education and Mike finished his degree in English and history. We decided to volunteer to work full time with migrant farm workers in camps we had visited as summer missionaries on the Eastern Shore of Virginia. After that, we would go to seminary. We wanted to become social workers to migrant workers and establish missions in border towns or perhaps go overseas. Our lives have turned out differently now, but I don't know how many people are still following the plans they made when they were twenty.

We went to Southern Seminary, a Baptist seminary in Louisville, Kentucky. It was about the time the denomination started turning to the right. We wanted to make a difference in people's lives, and we had been really involved with people. But when we got to seminary, we had to leave behind several important missionary points where God was clearly at work. Now we had to sit still and learn.

We ended up starting a Hispanic church in Louisville. Later we got a grant that paid us two hundred dollars a month. I don't know how we survived. By miracles.

Our son was born our first year of seminary, so we needed child care for him, which was a problem because the seminary's day care was expensive and at first they wouldn't accept any subsidies from the city. They saw this as an issue of separation of church and state. Without support, I was going to have to quit seminary. Then a friend told me that the city offered a subsidy for child care, so not knowing any different, I applied. The woman at the city agency told me the seminary day care didn't accept funding, but she said if they would allow an inspection, they could be certified. Somehow, she got an appointment with the day-care director. She came out to the day care, saw how wonderful it was, and certified the location so my son could be subsidized. That was a miracle! But after him, that was it. The day care didn't allow any others. I wish others had been approved. For us it was an answer to prayer. We paid sixty-seven dollars a month for his day care and the city subsidy paid the rest.

On the one hand there were the miracles, and on the other, lots of hurdles. The seminary had something called Seminary Days. It was designed to give student ministers a chance to preach in area churches. Mike and I both signed up. Mike got called four times in the first few months, but no calls came for me. I telephoned the seminary office to ask if they had lost my application and why I hadn't received any calls.

They said, "A church has to request a woman for us to send one."

I said, "Wait a minute. What do you mean they have to request a woman? I thought you just signed up for Seminary Days and they would call you."

They said, "No, they would have to request a woman."

I said, "Has anyone ever requested a woman?"

They said, "Yes, but it would be because a specific pastor or church knew to ask for you."

That meant I would have had to call all these church pastors and beg them to ask for me. Since we had come from missionary work, they didn't know me at all. The seminary then suggested I should look toward a position as minister of education. They said, "Do you play the piano?"

It was outrageous! Mike wrote a letter to the president of the seminary. This was after we had chaired the seminary student missions committee. Mike and I raised over $14,000 for missions. This made it possible to send kids on missions as far as China. I organized a challenge to the professors to see how much money they could raise. We were also in charge of a dorm. That's when I tried to create a food pantry for the dorms because I could see that some of the students were going hungry between paychecks. Jobs were hard to find. But my efforts were met with the comment that if seminarians were hungry it was because their wives were too lazy to go out and get work! I couldn't believe that! Some weren't even married to start with! This kind of assumption was so hard to believe. It was a terrible and a wonderful time.

The classes were fabulous. I gained so much respect for my professors. They had so much integrity, though many of them were run out because they were seen as being too liberal. So they became refugees of other denominations. For Mike it was horrible because he grew up Southern Baptist, and he was seeing how much the denomination was changing. It was hard to take.

I never did graduate from that seminary. Instead, I worked on a master's degree in education at the University of Louisville. When I graduated, I took a full-time job in education so Mike could finish his doctoral degree. Mike finished in 1991, at which point he took a teaching job at Bluefield College in Virginia. There were many things to love in Appalachia. I had a job teaching high school. Mike was working in something he loved, but we were desperate for challenges that were more intellectual and to grow professionally. Besides, in Bluefield, we always had to keep our opinions to ourselves and be closet liberals.

In 1994, we came to Chapel Hill for one year. We wanted to nurture our souls. We visited United Church of Chapel Hill and met Rick and Jill Edens. They were a real clergy couple, and it was great to see them serve together, and to be up front officiating together. It was also liberating to be able to talk about issues—abortion, integration, homosexuality—to speak about these subjects honestly. It was a wonderful experience.

In January 1995, in response to a very challenging sermon Jill preached calling us to reach out to the community, we started a Spanish Bible study at the church. Hispanic newcomers were hungry for fellowship and meaning, so we met here at United Church to study the Bible and from that formed a small ministry.

We did have to return to Bluefield for a year, but the Southern Conference of the United Church of Christ and I wrote up a proposal to the national United Church of Christ office to start a new church in Chapel Hill. I knew in my heart, and I said to our partners, that the plan the national church and Conference were suggesting wouldn't work. They wanted us to be self-sufficient within a five-year period. But there was no way that a church in a community with no established Hispanic presence could be self-supporting, not within the time frame the United Church of Christ had set up. North Carolina has one of the fastest growing Hispanic populations, but many of the people are transient; they have no resources, and in fact would be coming to us looking for help. That would make it doubly hard for us to become a self-sustaining church, but everybody wanted to see something started, so they said we'll work out the money part later. The one thing I learned about Americans is, you set a plan in motion, and that becomes the plan. There's not a lot of room for improvisation and changes; they want things done like your proposal says. That's what has brought us five years later to where we are today, which is, a pastor who will only be here part time and will be working full-time somewhere else.

Back in 1995, we were full of enthusiasm and willing to start with a ministry. Mike and I bought a house, moved in, and, in a week's time, had a vacation Bible school program. It was unbelievable what we were able to accomplish. I remember we had to start from scratch. Even the UCC logo wasn't available with Spanish words: *That they may all be one.* I wanted a Spanish manual for new members explaining who we are as a denomination, but there was nothing. A look at my shelves shows what we have from the United Church of Christ—very little! For my ordination service in 1997, I had to write the whole thing in Spanish and fax it to all my clergy friends for help. I was grateful to be approved for ordination into the United Church of Christ based on my two and a half years of seminary and my work in education, but I quickly saw how limited the United Church of Christ was going to be with Spanish support. The hymnal came out with some Spanish hymns and worship aids in 1999, but that is about the extent of it. I do have to say, the one area where the United Church of Christ has Spanish resources is asking people for money. That really makes me angry. The church needs to do more, much more. I have some Catholic resources for preaching. For Sunday school, I use materials from the Disciples of Christ church. For children I use a Methodist curriculum that is on a three-year cycle. The only problem is our children have all been through it, and now there is nothing new for them. From El Paso, Texas, you can get an abundance of material from the right-wing conservatives, but it is nothing we want to use! Of course, we don't have money for resources—never had. That's hard, especially when you see the Anglo churches spend thousands. They throw away more unused material than we are able to purchase. I dream of one day having a budget to buy books and more. You know how much we spent for our church retreat? Two hundred and ten dollars, including the cabins, plus ten dollars for food per family.

The faith my congregation exhibits is inspiring. Some people have amazing stories of survival and courage. They take care of their families back home while working two jobs here and doing without so many things that we consider indispensable. So many people don't appreciate or even know the tremendous contributions immigrants make. I wish I could highlight them all!

For me, preaching and doing the service is really important, though sometimes I really don't want to come to church because I feel the weight of the injustices. Then we have the service, and it is wonderful to be in a community of faith. It strengthens me and makes me glad that I'm the pastor. Church is something my spirit needs. But it is hard to worship when the rest of the week feels like there's little reason to praise God. It's more like, God, where are you? But the discipline of doing what the Bible says brings amazing results. *Count your blessings,* or *praise the Lord,* didn't make sense to me while being faced with so much injustice, but as I get older and just do what the Bible says, I understand. Sometimes you just have to follow what God says and later you understand why. Thanksgiving is an attitude, independent of circumstances.

My favorite part of ministry is to visit with people in their homes and lead Bible study. Visiting in someone's home is bringing a taste of God's grace into his or her household. I only wish my visits didn't conflict so much with homework and putting my own children to bed. I have three children and they all require attention. I am always stretched thin, and I know that sometimes it makes me grumpy. My family has to sacrifice a lot.

Pastoral counseling is one of my difficulties. It is so easy as an outsider to see what other people should do, but then I realize how hard it is. I know the barriers they face.

I hate the administrative work in the church and the time that it takes, like doing the bulletin. I'm not good at finances, either. I wish I had members who were good at that sort of thing. If I could only import my aunt who was a president of a parent-teacher association in Peru, she would know what to do. I need to figure out how to fill these sorts of leadership roles. Iglesia folks work two or more jobs, and most have never been part of a congregational church. We need so much training.

As for the future of my ministry, we will continue to have worship services and Bible study; we will be a community of faith, but my time will become limited. Now I do so much for my church members and others who are desperate for help. I translate at Social Services, at parent-teacher conferences, at the doctor. I guess I won't be able to do that so much now that our funding has dried up, but how to be fair about splitting my time between the church and my family? I know if someone calls me in the middle of the night with a need, that I will go, part-time or not. If that is what you call ministry, then that is what I do.

My husband thinks I work eighty hours a week. I don't think so, but I am always doing something; sometimes I'm still up at one o'clock in the morning doing church work or catching up on housework, but I wouldn't trade the last six years for anything. Not even a retirement account with real money in it. I guess I'll have to wait to see my treasures in heaven.

# SIMPLE VESSEL, ABUNDANT GRACE

## JULIE PEEPLES

On a weekend trip in the mountains in the fall of 1976, my college roommates and I stopped at a small roadside pottery studio. As we made our way through rows of beautiful pieces, I spotted a simple clay chalice, fired in earth tones, on a small table off to the side. There was nothing extraordinary about it; the light beige around the cup was spotted with darker flecks, a simple curving line had been etched into the widest portion. The base and lower part of the cup had been glazed a dark brown. I was not much of a shopper and had very little spare cash, but I knew I had to buy the chalice; it was almost as though it was there just for me. So I handed over my last twenty, taking the two dollars in change. As we drove back to school, I held the chalice and knew with absolute certainty that one day I would be using that piece in worship, in leading a service of communion.

It was an assurance I needed. Having been born and raised in a Catholic family, I had told few people of the call I sensed, a call I believed then would result in my ordination as a priest. From my teenage years on, I had watched the priests celebrating the mass and knew somewhere in my being that I was meant to do that. I was so sure of this that I assumed the change would not be long in coming, that the pope would simply wake up one morning and, realizing the error, clear the way for women like me to be ordained. The few people I shared this with either stared at me in silence or urged me to consider joining a convent instead, believing I would only get into trouble otherwise. Eventually I did find spiritual support and friendship with an order of sisters who took me under their wing for a while. At one point, I wrote to the bishop of my diocese to let him know my plans and to request a meeting with him. He refused in no uncertain terms and suggested I go away.

While in college I became intrigued by my first exposure to Protestant thought and history, largely through the marvelous religion faculty and chaplains at Furman University during that time. The concept of "the priesthood of all believers" was utterly new and wonderful for me. Still, I believed change was on its way in the Catholic Church.

Following college and after teaching for a year in a Catholic elementary school, in the fall of 1980, I headed to seminary at Andover Newton Theological School in Newton, Massachusetts, which had been highly recommended by the religion department at Furman. There I could, and eventually would, take courses at three Catholic seminaries in the Boston area. In one of those courses, I walked in on the first day of class and took a seat, the only female in the class. The half dozen or so male seminarians already there promptly picked up their notebooks and moved to the other side of the room, away from me. Ironically, it was a course in ethics. There were other Catholics at Andover Newton, both on staff and in the student body; together we held on to the hope that the church would soon clear the way for women to be ordained, even with growing evidence to the contrary. Maria Harris taught Christian education there at the time and was an engaging source of inspiration for many of us who refused to let go of our hope and our calling.

While in seminary I served at a Franciscan shrine and at a homeless shelter for women, Rosie's Place. Both were challenging and valuable experiences for me. My supervisor was from the shrine; the Reverend Chris Keenan was a wonderful source of support, mentoring, and friendship in those years. Having grown up in Charleston, South Carolina, I had had no experience of life in a large urban setting. My first glimpse of homeless women and men spreading pieces of cardboard across ventilation grates on the sidewalks to sleep on is forever etched in my mind. That shock led to my work with the shelter as part of my seminary training. The colorful characters that used Rosie's Place as a home base impacted my understanding of ministry in ways that books and lectures could not. The heart-wrenching blend of dignity and degradation those women lived gave me an invaluable lesson about human nature and the complexities involved in wanting to serve others. And while I thought I was well-informed about racism, I was not prepared for the forms of racism I encountered in the North. The most graphic lesson came on Easter Sunday night in 1981, when I found myself caught in the middle of a racial riot on a subway. In spite of my own naïveté, I escaped unharmed, thanks to several police officers who escorted me to safety.

Like many others, I worked my way through seminary, and as a result met my future husband, the Reverend Paul Davis, who supervised the kitchen crew I was assigned to. A week after our graduation, we married on campus and then drove off for Pittsburgh, where Paul would serve as pastor of an American Baptist congregation and I accepted a position as a campus minister at a small Catholic college in a nearby town.

That experience proved pivotal. The head of the campus ministry department was a priest whom I would later learn had strongly resisted hiring a woman, but was forced to do so because the college had recently become coeducational. I would also come to learn that he was involved in several inappropriate relationships with students. When my efforts at confronting him and then bringing the matter to two administrators got nowhere, I decided to leave at the end of the school year. Although the administrators had initially told me they were aware of the problems with this priest and thanked me for coming forward, they later refused to pursue the matter. I realized through the painful experience that I would always be at risk—responsibility with no authority, always at the mercy of a priest who may or may not accept my presence. I quickly decided that to stay in the Catholic Church for me would be self-abusive. It would take a bit longer for me to accept that I was not "leaving God" by leaving the church in which I had been raised; it would take longer still to resolve the guilt I felt over not staying in and "fighting the good fight" on behalf of women in the church.

We returned to Massachusetts, where I decided to align with the United Church of Christ, in large part because of the kinship I had felt with UCC folk at Andover Newton. In 1985, I accepted the position of minister of family life at a large UCC church north of Boston. While I often felt lost in the crowd of the large established church, there were two other women on staff who became my first real mentors as women in ministry, another invaluable experience. I was ordained in 1988.

In the early spring of 1989, Paul and I accepted calls to be the first chaplains for Habitat for Humanity International at the headquarters in Americus, Georgia. I had long wanted to head back south, and Paul was ready for a change as well. We both admired Habitat and jumped at the chance to become part of the organization. In many ways, it was the most wonderful opportunity we could ever imagine: work that we believed in, the chance to develop further as ministers, an environment filled with people of all "ages and stages" who shared a commitment to living their faith and living simply. I learned so very much from the men, women, and children we encountered. Part of our ministry was to work with and lead retreats for people serving in Habitat's international settings, so we even had opportunities to travel and to see other cultures.

Still, the dream had a darker side. We heard stories through exit interviews, numerous stories, of inappropriate behavior on the part of a key Habitat figure. We came to the decision that we would have to confront the person involved, and shared our plan with another top leader. We were warned against this course of action, as others before us had apparently tried to do the same and "were no longer with the organization." Instead, we took our concerns to two trusted board members and sought their help. The matter was soon out of our hands. An investigation ensued in which the charges were found to be true; some changes were made. Unfortunately in the end, we lost our jobs along with others who had become involved along the way. The first to be fired were our dear friends David and Bonnie Rowe, who had worked diligently for the organization since its early days. What had started out as a private matter had become public without our intending it to be so, and in the end, all of us who had tried to work for significant changes were forced to leave. A painful ending, but the lessons learned were many and the experience itself still yields treasured memories and lasting friendships.

When our time in Americus came to an end, Paul and I, now with our two young daughters Meghan and Hannah, played the game of "whoever gets a decent job first wins." We wanted to stay in the South, if possible, and we traveled through the Southeast and Southern Conferences interviewing. Those I met with in the Southern Conference were less than encouraging, painting a bleak but honest picture of the prospects for a woman. Following up one last lead, I spoke with the search committee at Congregational UCC in Greensboro, who were looking for an interim director of Christian education. We set up an interview, during the course of which they informed me they were also looking for an interim pastor and thought I might be best suited for that. After an interview with the pastoral search committee, I was offered the interim position and we moved to Greensboro in early October of 1991, not knowing how long this would last.

From the moment I set foot on the grounds of Congregational UCC, I had a deep and abiding sense of being where I belonged, if only for a brief time. There was a rightness about it that made all the hard work seem easier. For the year-and-a-half interim period, we worked together, the congregation and I, processing the conflict that had taken place there in recent years, sorting through, sharing stories, reworking what hadn't worked, praying, laughing, and crying together. Toward the end of the interim period, they began asking if I would stay. My answer was immediate and definite: No. I had agreed to be an interim and it was not right to stay. They kept asking, and for a long time my answer remained the same. Finally, after much prayer and consulting with people I respected both in and outside the church, I agreed to consider the possibility. The search committee and I developed with the congregation an open, above-board process for all to consider the possibility of my being called as the permanent senior minister. In the end, in May of 1993, the formal call was issued, the vote taken, and I accepted. As my colleague and friend the Reverend Arnie Johnson stated then, "sometimes you have to put your principles aside and do the right thing."

My years at Congregational have been filled with the trials and tribulations, endless surprises and profound joys that can come from this strange partnership of pastor and congregation. It has been a time of great healing and grace for me, strengthened by the blessing of seeing how an infinitely creative God takes strands of very diverse texture, color and length and weaves something whole and even beautiful. Never would I have thought that I would be a Protestant pastor and preacher, introvert and former Catholic that I am. Yet, I have come to marvel at the wonder of a group of people committing, through worship and service and simple human compassion, to becoming a community of living faith. Discerning God's leading, I have asked the congregation to take risks and they have responded with courage. During my tenure here, several close family members have endured serious illnesses and I have experienced the loss of my parents. The congregation has cared for me and for my family, helping me learn how to receive such care in the difficult times. Together we have lived through the pain of losing some incredibly wonderful saints through death, we have cried tears of joy at the baptisms of infants born to parents who had given up hope, we have studied scripture and been amazed to learn we really can welcome all God's people and live to tell the tale and love one another all the more.

One particular turning point came in October of 1995, with the very unexpected death of a man who had been a strong leader in the church and in the wider community. The shock of John Kernodle's death had a profound effect on many of us; his loss left a huge empty space that no one else could fill. I knew better than to even try to fill it, yet I also sensed a responsibility to carry on something of his spirit, his vision. That marked for me a significant increase in my community involvement, first in the school system (John was chair of the county board of education at the time of his death) and then in various interfaith efforts. The example of his integrity and his compassion inspire me still.

I have used my simple chalice so many times I have lost count: a small communion service with other women in Massachusetts, breaking bread with coworkers on retreat on a Guatemalan hillside, in worship at Congregational. On those days when I wonder why I do what I do and how it all came to be, I glance over to the small table in my study where it sits. I do not know where else this sojourn may take us, but I am learning all the while to trust the One who pours out abundant grace from very simple vessels.

# MARY'S JOURNEY

**Congregational United Church of Christ**
**Greensboro, North Carolina**
**December 21, 2003**

JULIE PEEPLES

SCRIPTURE: Luke 1:39-55

If there was a census today as there was in that time, if you had to travel back to the place of your birth to be registered as Joseph and Mary did, how far would you have to go? Who would have to travel the farthest here? Where would you have to go? I would have to go to Charleston. Milwaukee? That's pretty good. Green Bay? Wesley Long Hospital? You could walk—no sympathy! Did someone say Atlanta? China?

Well, the journey Mary and Joseph took down from Nazareth to Bethlehem would have been some eighty miles. And nine months pregnant, whether by donkey or by foot would not have been a pleasant journey. I can remember both of our trips to the hospital by car with a caffeine-deprived driver, and neither of those was particularly pleasant, so eighty miles at the end stage of pregnancy, I'm sure they had some good stories to tell. But the more intriguing journey, it seems to me, is Mary's spiritual journey. That is not one they would have talked about in that time, but it is very interesting to me. How would what supposedly would have been a very young woman of no means, no formal education, no real prospects for anything in life have come to the point where she could pour forth this incredible song of praise and confidence? And yes, it echoes the song of Hannah, the mother of Samuel, and parts of the psalms, so they were familiar words she was reaching into and bringing up. But still, how could this young, uneducated, poor woman have just burst forth with this? What was going on in her that could lead her to do this, to say these things? Something was stirred up here! Where was that coming from, and what would it take for us to discover ourselves on a similar journey to get to that point? To sound so amazingly confident in what God was up to and accomplishing in the world and our part in it? How did she get there? Clearly, Mary knew some things.

Well, for one thing, Mary knew her history. Not like we know history. We know the dates, facts, and the figures, and if we're lucky, we know some of the grand sweeping movements of history. But Mary knew her story, her people's story, how they had gone from being nobody to being a people that God had somehow redeemed. They had been this nobody, nothing slave people destined for absolute extinction in Egypt's land and God had taken pity on them and had come to their aid and had used Moses to set them free from Pharaoh's rule. God had given them a land and a name, an identity, a future. Mary had been raised since early childhood to know that story by heart. It had been passed on by word of mouth year after year. That was their story, their family history, as if you could take out a picture album and turn page after page: "Yes, there's Moses and there's Miriam and yes, this is the part when they crossed the Red Sea . . . yes, this is what happened when they settled in the land" and so on. It was her story. She knew her past. She knew God was not one to patiently wait for people just to die out in the wilderness. She knew her history. She knew that over and over again people had broken the covenant, had turned away, they had blown it; still God had called them back. She knew that at times her people had been oppressed, had been stepped upon as if they were nothing, only to have God come to their aid again. She knew this by heart. That is what Mary knew. Always, always, God had been faithful, no matter what. No matter what—God was there. This she knew.

She knew also what was happening in the here and now, what was happening in the present. She only had to look around to know that now Israel was an occupied land, that Rome was their landlord. The religious leaders of her time were in collusion with Rome, often selling out to Rome. The poor were getting poorer, the rich were getting richer off the backs of the poor, off the suffering of others. She only had to look around to see that that was true, to look and see the growing divisions between those deemed worthy and those considered unworthy. The line was clearly drawn between the clean and the unclean, a separation between those whose money was worth something and whose was not. It didn't take anyone with a formal education to see the way things were heading.

But now, Mary knew something more. Now, something else was added to the equation. God was working through her life now. God was doing something unimaginable. Unbelievable. Unthinkable. Incredible. But hadn't God always done things in a strange, surprising, peculiar way? Hadn't God chosen an uncharted path before? Build an ark, Noah. Go to a land I'll show you, Abraham. Climb up this mountain, Moses. Hadn't God always broken precedents? Surely, God was doing that now. A child will be born to you, Mary, who will be the Savior of the world. God was now using Mary's life, weaving Mary's story into this great whole. And so with this full and overflowing heart, Mary just burst forth with this praise, this dance, this song. Just confident, just so confident that she puts it in terms that it had already happened. God has sent the rich away empty. God has filled up the stomachs of the hungry. It's done. If they'd had that phrase two thousand years ago, she would have used it: it's a done deal, folks, we've won. The suffering's over. God's done it. That's how confident, how sure she felt.

How do we join Mary's journey? Do we dare join Mary's journey? In truth, we're already part of Mary's journey. We're already part of it! Because that story, that's our story. That's our story too. We know that story. Even if we've never thought of it as ours. It's ours. How God led Moses and the people out of slavery, out of captivity to freedom. How time and time again people through all of history have blown it, have turned away from the covenant, have acted as if they didn't need God, could get along better on their own, thank you very much. We don't need the demands, we'll do fine by ourselves. Only they found they couldn't, so God draws them back in. Only to find out the story of slavery is one that gets repeated over and over again, and God steps in again and again to say, "No. That is not how I have designed this world. That is not how you are to live with one another." We know that history. It is our history.

The one constant throughout is God's faithfulness to the covenant. Like Mary, we know, don't we, modern-day pharaohs? They don't all come out of spider holes. Some of them are still walking around in palaces and fancy government buildings. We battle Herods in halls of power and on smaller scales wherever one person or one group uses power over others in a way that dehumanizes, that labels, oppresses, denies full humanity, draws that line back and says no, you belong on this side and those others belong on that side. Some people are clean and some are not, some are worthy and some are not. That's when you've got the Herods and the pharaohs and we know, we know them.

A couple of weeks ago in my sermon, I confessed that I wished God would go back to smiting, just go ahead and smite a few people. I've got my list ready. Some of you since then have said to me, "I've got a few names, can I add them to your list?" Don't get me started, because my list has grown since then! It sometimes seems the bad guys are winning and it's hard to keep hoping. It's hard to understand where Mary got that confidence to say it's a done deal. But you see the story's not over. Because there's this baby who was born in a manger who by all rights shouldn't have even lived. And God is still doing amazing, unbelievable, risky things, weaving our stories in with this great story, taking our tragedies and our tears, our struggles and our joys, our best efforts and our shining victories, our humiliating failures and our defeats, and weaving them all together into this colorful whole. Mary's journey didn't end in that stable, and it didn't end at Calvary, it kept on going. Our journeys are shaped by the tragedies and by the victories, but they are not defined by them. We are part of a greater story and a much, much longer journey, the end of which we may not live to see. We may not be able to speak with the same courage and confidence that Mary could, but we live with the same sure hope that God who freed a slave people frees them still today and will continue to free them tomorrow. That all shall be reconciled. This is what WE know. That God has the ultimate last word. "The wolf and the lamb shall feed together. . . . They shall not hurt or destroy on all my holy mountain," says God. That is what we celebrate this Christmas. And it shall be so. Amen.

# LOVER AND NURTURER OF THE INSTITUTIONAL CHURCH

## CALLY ROGERS-WITTE

ake my life and let it be consecrated, Lord, to thee...." I remember the words of the hymns we sang at summer church camp when I was in the tenth grade. I certainly wasn't thinking of ordained ministry, having never known a female ordained minister, and probably not even of a career in the church, but we were focusing on the varied talents and gifts that God had given each of us and how we were asked to use those talents for good. I specifically remember a counselor pointing out that the more gifts (such as intelligence, supportive family life, material wealth, musical ability) that we were given, the more we were expected to use those gifts in the service of God's love. Those words fit with what my parents had taught and modeled all my life. So, although I couldn't articulate the theology back then, it has always been about God's mission, not mine; it has been Christ's ministry, not mine, to which I am called. My very life is a gift I have been given for the sole purpose of offering it back to God in loving service. The first time I heard about "stewardship of life" that theme resonated with me! Of course, I have fallen short, again and again, and my early prayers were always laden with confession ("God, I'm so sorry I was mean to my mother!") even as now I try very hard to focus on thanksgiving in my prayers and tried to teach my two daughters to give thanks every night rather than to focus on guilt.

My earliest interests were political as I saw the social, economic, and political spheres of life as the place to try to "make a difference," to do the largest amount of "good" for the most number of people, to try to create a society based on God's principles of justice, equality, peace, and love. At Mary Baldwin College, a church-related women's college in Virginia, I originally majored in political science, but after spending my junior year in France, I switched during my senior year to a major in religion and philosophy (in my mind the other major with the most interesting and challenging classes) when our only poli-sci professor left the college and was replaced by someone I didn't know. Looking back, I can see that switch as only one example of the many times when God led me toward ordained ministry without my even realizing it. Thinking I didn't want to get engaged and married right after college like so many of my classmates, I decided to go to graduate school, but I was too naive to know the difference between going to graduate school in religion and going to seminary, so I ended up at Yale University's divinity school in the two-year master of arts in religion program. I think I believed I would eventually teach or do social work, but I certainly did not expect to be ordained or to work professionally in the church.

It was 1967. I chose Yale because it had enough female students (10 percent) to have a small women's dorm. I loved the academic challenge and was fascinated by my studies, especially the beginnings of Latin American and African American liberation theology as well as the classes on Tillich, Niebuhr, and Bultmann. I did my two years of field work in places that awakened me (sheltered southern "young lady" that I had been) to the racial justice struggles of our time: working with teens at Dixwell Avenue Congregational Church, a predominantly black congregation, and, the second year, with the Fair Housing Center of the

Urban League of New Haven. Those experiences continued my "political conversion" from being a Goldwater conservative to a political liberal, which had begun at Mary Baldwin in classes on the Hebrew prophets and their call for social justice.

I jumped at the opportunity to go back to my beloved France in 1969, as director of Christian education at the American Church in Paris (even though I had never had even one Christian education class—but they assumed that since I was a female I surely knew all about Sunday school and youth ministry). What I found out in those two years was that, to my surprise, I very much liked "church work" and that I did, indeed, want to be involved in all aspects of a church's life, not simply education. So, after one more year in New Haven working full-time in fair housing (as well as part-time in Christian education at Yale's Battell Chapel where I first encountered the United Church of Christ), I applied to Pacific School of Religion (PSR) in Berkeley, California, to finish work toward a master of divinity. All of my life experiences so far seemed to point me in the direction of ordination (I have always felt as if I was "pushed and shoved" into my call to ministry, rather than pulled). One more life experience prepared me to be a more caring, empathetic pastor than I could have been without it: during the years in New Haven and Paris, I was in a very unhappy marriage that ended in divorce. Up until that time I had never really known suffering firsthand.

The decision to go to PSR (rather than a half-dozen other seminaries I investigated) was very intuitive, based more on the sunshine, Bay Area, eucalyptus trees and "feeling of community with students and professors" than the coursework, but I soon learned that I loved the classes too! At PSR, I concentrated on "practical" courses to really prepare me for church leadership: counseling, preaching, Bible study, worship, and Christian education. The opportunity to take courses at several of the other Graduate Theological Union's seminaries was a real plus—sexuality education with the Unitarians, preaching with the Presbyterians, and a class on Teilhard de Chardin with the Jesuits. Another exciting "new thing" that God was suddenly doing at that time was calling more women to ministry, so my entering class at PSR had almost 50 percent females, which was a real joy. Reading and talking about issues of women's liberation made theology come even more alive for me personally. I got to put into practice some of my learnings about small groups, counseling, and creative worship through my field education placement at Arlington Community Church (United Christ of Christ) in Kensington, California, where I was ordained on December 1, 1973.

Three weeks later, in my parents' living room back in Rockledge, Florida, Frank Benedetto Witte and I were married, after a long-distance courtship, beginning our lifelong love, "best friendship," and adventure. We hyphenated our names and moved our few belongings to Chapel Hill, North Carolina, where he was enrolled in graduate school to become a clinical psychologist. Before moving, I had visited several churches in central North Carolina (of various denominations) to offer my services as a minister. The nondenominational Community Church of Chapel Hill offered me an unpaid "call" that got me ordained. The church had a UCC minister who turned out to be a wonderful "boss" and true colleague for me at that time (quite a change from the senior ministers and employers who had treated me as a "second-class citizen" in Paris and New Haven). I supplemented our meager income by leading "growth groups" and marriage enrichment classes and teaching parenting classes (a real stretch for someone with no kids!). When Frank decided to go to school full-time, I needed to look for full-time paid employment and God "pushed" me once again to the right place at the right time!

I went to work for the almost brand new national Office for Church Life and Leadership (OCLL) of the United Church of Christ whose executive, the Reverend Reuben Sheares, was a fantastic mentor! Several of the staff members were regionally deployed, so I was assigned to the southern region and my office was located in a former classroom at Pilgrim United Church of Christ in Durham. I don't think I have ever learned so much in a two-year time period in my life. I remember my first OCLL staff meeting with all the UCC "alphabet soup" names for church organizations and the many polity mysteries. I came back home to tell Frank that "I felt like I was in a foreign country where I loved the people and the customs but I didn't speak the language!" The Office for Church Life and Leadership had responsibility for helping the whole church with issues related to ordained and lay leadership, theology, worship, theological education, and women's concerns. That agency, created to be collaborative and collegial, foreshadowed much that is good in the new UCC national restructuring. My colleagues on that staff have continued to be some of my best role models and friends throughout my ministry. But, the advent of a very happily welcomed but unplanned baby in 1977 meant that I couldn't continue such a travel schedule for too many more years, although little Mary Ann did take fifty-six airplane trips before the age of nine months!

Again, with God's "push," I was called to what I had long thought was "the most wonderful UCC congregation in the southern region" and which I later believed was the most wonderful church in the entire country (yes, I do tend to exaggerate about almost everything), Community United Church of Christ, in Raleigh, North Carolina. Community United Church of Christ (CUCC) had a long tradition of standing up for racial and social justice. It was said to be "the first public place where blacks and whites could sit down to a meal together in Raleigh" at the church's annual Institute of Religion, begun in the 1930s, which brought to town nationally acclaimed speakers and classes every winter. The church paired with predominantly African American churches to be the first to integrate the state park system with a joint summer church camp and established a low-income apartment complex and an early integrated day-care center. By the early 1980s, it was natural for CUCC to take the lead in a citywide effort to reduce the nuclear arms race with the "Raleigh Peace Initiative" and later to welcome refugees from Central America as they fled persecution in their homeland and journeyed toward a new life in Canada. A byproduct of the congregation's witness for justice and peace was a slow but steady growth in numbers, dollars, and spirit. We certainly didn't do anything intentional about "the scary E word," evangelism, while I was pastor at CUCC, something I feel badly about now as I have learned the importance of words as well as deeds to invite people to the fullness of life in the love of Christ.

We were growing in other arenas too. Our family added a second precious daughter, Beth, and moved from a condominium to a house with a backyard. The church began to be more intentional about its use of inclusive language to speak about humans and about God. And it focused more clearly on the two-sided call to "nurture personal faith AND work for social justice" as it offered more prayer groups and support groups for growth in faith as well as opportunities for social activism. (Later, in keeping with the times, the slogan was changed to "nurturing spiritual growth and working for social justice.") Community United Church of Christ also became the first "ONA" congregation in the Southern Conference, church number 35 on the list of Open and Affirming UCC churches that welcome the gifts of persons without regard to their sexual orientation. At the time, that vote by the congregation seemed to come embarrassingly late, although now it is counted among the "early" ONA churches. The church was well-prepared for that positive vote by its longtime hosting (since 1976) in its building of St. John's, the local congregation of the Universal Fellowship of Metropolitan Community Churches, which has a special mission in the gay and lesbian community. Several members of CUCC also gave early leadership to the Raleigh Religious Network for Gay and Lesbian Equality (with Nancy Keppel being the "pusher" and catalyst for that justice ministry and many others!).

That congregation really taught me how to be a pastor and how to work for justice during those eighteen years. It also taught me the importance of being a community of faith, not just a social or political organization. The church encouraged my participation in the wider ministry of the church, through my years of service on the UCC Executive Council, the governing board of the National Council of Churches, and the North Carolina Council of Churches. Members of CUCC were instrumental in founding an ecumenical organization called CLAY (Clergy and Laity Together in Ministry), which offered church members the opportunity to explore the relationship between their faith and their call to ministry (whether it be volunteer ministry, lay ministry, commissioned or ordained). In one of those sessions of "Faith to Focused Ministry," we were asked to list all the various "hats" that we each wore. My list included, of course, wife, mother, daughter, pastor, organizer, cheerleader (a holdover from high school that served me well when I was a pastor), and "lover and nurturer of the institutional church." I was surprised when I wrote that last one down. As a child of the 1960s, somehow I didn't expect to become a leader of the "institutional" church; I thought I would be a "change agent." But as I explored that "hat," I realized that my deep love for the United Church of Christ sprang precisely from its historic work for social justice motivated by a deep faith in a God who "so loves the world," the whole world with all its inhabitants, and its choice of the prayer of Jesus, "that they may all be one," as its denominational motto.

Answering the call to become the Conference minister of the Southwest Conference of the United Church of Christ in 1995 seemed to flow out of that role of loving and nurturing the institutional church, but the physical move from Raleigh to Phoenix, Arizona, did not flow as naturally! Frank was well-established in private practice in central Carolina and probably expected to stay there until retirement. I was certainly not "searching" for a new position; it came out of the blue. Daughter Mary Ann was finishing her senior year in high school at the time of my new call, but Beth was only in ninth grade. Upon hearing the news that I was the candidate of the search committee to become the Conference minister of the Southwest Conference, Beth gave me a big hug and exclaimed, "Oh, Mommy, I'm so proud of you, and I want you to know that I'm not going to move!" But she did; we all did, although Mary Ann quickly moved back to North Carolina to attend Elon College. Frank amazingly supported what we both experienced as a genuine call from God (why else would we uproot our whole life and move across country?!). For several years after our move, every time I said, "I love you," to him, he replied, "You should!" He missed his colleagues, his clients, his contacts, the ocean, every aspect of his life "back East." Now, however, thank God (and I do!), he says "Thank you for moving me out here" as he enjoys immensely his new work as organizational consultant and executive coach for upper-level management in large companies. Much of that work is done in and out of San Diego so he even has an ocean back in his life. The hard part is that he travels during the week and I travel or am tied up most weekends, so we have to grab precious time together when we can. I love this work, but I am glad I am doing it at this stage of my life and not when our children were younger. The intense travel schedule and the sixty-five-to-seventy hour (on average!) work weeks of Conference ministry would not be possible for me combined with being a mother of youngsters. As I look back on the years in Raleigh, I am grateful to Community UCC for having allowed me to reduce my time from full-time to three-quarters when my children were in school so that I had the summers free for parenting and a bit more flexibility in my daily schedule. I am especially grateful to God and the congregation for calling the Reverend David Barber to be our associate pastor and my wonderful colleague in ministry during the second half of those years at CUCC. There was a very special synergy in the combination of our exceptionally different personalities, gifts, and experiences with our shared theological affirmations and mutual respect.

Pastoral ministry is such a unique blessing and privilege—I loved being involved in people's lives at moments of great meaning, at births and deaths, and I loved being so integrally involved in a community of faith. Planning and leading worship and working together for justice were enormously fulfilling ways to use my time and talent. Conference ministry is fascinating with its great variety and immense challenges in this anti-authority and anti-institutional era when "spirituality" is appreciated but "religion" is not. Conference ministry can be especially exhausting and draining, but I feel personally revitalized by the beauty of the Southwest as I travel to visit churches in Arizona, New Mexico, and El Paso, Texas. The first several years here were close to overwhelming with all the competing demands for my time and energy and the "heaviness" of some aspects of the work (especially churches in conflict, churches in serious decline, or complex issues relating to church and ministry such as misconduct allegations), but God's gift of the glorious sunrises, sunsets, and landscapes in this part of the country sustained me each day. I found my daily spiritual disciplines more important than ever, and more "stripped down and basic" than ever, as I asked simply for "the daily bread" to get through this day. Part of my experience of my original call to Conference ministry was the belief that God promised to give me the resources necessary to do the work (for I surely have never felt that I had sufficient resources myself to do this challenging ministry!). It's up to me to remember to rely on those resources and to put my trust in God each day! In the fall of 2000, I took a much-needed sabbatical, which emphasized "being" more than "doing." For a month, I was immersed in Mexican culture and trying to learn Spanish in beautiful Morelia and Guadalajara, followed by three glorious months of reading more novels than work-related books and copying all my longtime family recipes as a Christmas gift for my daughters. Since returning from that sabbatical, I have felt more at peace in this role and find myself enjoying it more than ever. It still often seems like "an impossible job," but I have relaxed into it a bit more these past several years. As a "small membership/large geography conference," our financial resources are severely stretched. Lacking the ability to have an associate conference minister, we have devised a very creative (if sometimes chaotic) staffing pattern that includes a number of part-time associate colleagues with whom I delight in working!

One of the real joys of Conference ministry is the opportunity to get to know so many marvelous people. I cherish the time with colleagues from around the country at various meetings and I feel privileged to get to read all those profiles about the faith journeys and theology of ministry of so many special persons. We are especially gifted with exceptionally faithful and talented clergy in the Southwest, and I delight in the number of women God has called into ordained ministry that the whole United Church of Christ is now celebrating as well! We are just beginning to see the blessing that gay, lesbian, bisexual, and transgendered leaders will be to the church. The United Church of Christ is fortunate to be on the receiving end of the gifts of so many wonderful persons who might not have been accepted as church leaders even a generation ago.

It is God's magnificent mission in which we are invited to participate! It is the very ministry of Christ to which we are called. It is the church, the very body of Christ, where we are asked to take leadership. Thanks be to God!

# INVITE EVERYONE!

⊞

CALLY ROGERS-WITTE

**SCRIPTURE: Matthew 22:1-14**

*This sermon was written to be preached in congregations around the Southwest Conference (SWC), United Church of Christ, in the late 1990s, to inspire faithful congregational visioning in my early years in the SWC. Much of what is said here I learned from the faithful members at Community UCC in Raleigh, North Carolina, as well as in congregations across the Southwest Conference.*

"Many are called, but few are chosen." What are we to make of this rather strange story that Jesus told to explain what the realm of God is like? The realm of God is like a king who gave a wedding party for his son and sent out invitations to all the fancy folks, but they wouldn't come. So the king had his servants go back to the people whom he had invited and tell them what a *fabulous* party it was going to be, and still they would not come, "they made light of it and went away, one to his farm, another to his business," and the rest treated his servants shamefully! So the king, after a huge burst of anger and retribution, *invited anyone and everyone to the party*—just go out into the streets and bring them in, the homeless, the poor, the sinners, *and* the "fancy folk," "the good folk," everybody! But then, when one of these poor folks came in and didn't have on the proper clothes, the king had that person *arrested* and tied up! "For many are called, but few are chosen." *What are we to make of this strange story?* . . .

The story is a *metaphor;* it's told to evoke a feeling, to help us understand the incomprehensible realm of God. I was most helped by the words of Fred Craddock, retired professor of preaching, who wrote,

> God's invitation is most gracious; ALL are invited, both bad and good. (We can breathe a sigh of relief—ALL are invited into God's realm, no matter what!) But just because all are *invited* does not mean that there are no standards, no *expectations* of the guests. A *"wedding garment"* is *"expected"*—now the "wedding garment" is the metaphor or symbol for "new life," for "right behavior, changed conduct." God invites us all; AND we are expected to *respond* with the same generosity, grace, and love that God shows to us!

The "realm of God" is a picture of what God wants the whole world to be like—God wants everyone to come willingly and joyfully to the beautiful party of life, wearing the appropriate clothes of love and kindness, clothed in reconciliation and compassion, sharing and caring, giving thanks for the goodness of God and acting like persons who have indeed been blessed by God! The early Christians, who heard and then told and retold this fascinating story, must have applied it to what the *church* was *supposed* to be like, as a microcosm of this "realm of God" to which all are invited and in which certain responses are expected.

In my new capacity as your Conference minister, I have had many occasions to contemplate what our graceful and grace-filled God expects of us as "church." We are all invited, I believe that; so what *are* the appropriate "clothes" to wear, what does church "look like" in these last days of the twentieth century?

What is "church" to you? I have—in my mind—not just ONE "picture of the church," but lots of pictures, images, snapshots almost, of "church"; I bet you do too.

"*Church*" to me, for example, is all the people who came to my mother's funeral in my hometown in Florida seven years ago—they packed into that sanctuary—we had to set up folding chairs, and they all had stories to tell me after the service, of what she had meant to them, of how she had been the one to listen, to understand, to reach out, to help. They shared tears with me; they shared laughter with me. They remembered how she had taught the preschool class and a parenting class for young parents. That was surely "church" to me.

"*Church*" is also the group of people in the congregation I served back in North Carolina who every third Sunday of the month came together to cook spaghetti or a pot of stew, and to chop up vegetables and fruit, and to bake cookies, and to take all that food downtown to the shelter for homeless folks, and who served the food, and tried to engage in conversation with their dinner guests, and washed the dishes alongside some of those they had fed; and the folks who stayed overnight at that shelter, once a month, especially the man who brought along little miniature chocolate bars to put out on the pillows of the cots after he made up the beds for the folks who would sleep there that night! That's church for me. Be *hospitable* to everyone!

"*Church*" is also singing a favorite hymn with tears streaming down my face because of all the memories it brings back and because of the grace and forgiveness that song literally wraps around me, just when I need it most. That's church—*everyone* is loved and forgiven!

"*Church*" is the small group that meets together every Thursday night during Lent to share their pain, loneliness, fears, hopes, and small successes, and to pray together; they used to meet in a Sunday school room, but now they meet in the home of a member of the group whose degenerative disease won't let her get outside of her own home anymore, but whose incredible spirit of love and joy is contagious for the others in the group and no one would miss a meeting. *Invite everyone*, not just the able bodied.

"*Church*" is even a fight at a congregational meeting over the budget, or some building renovation plan, painful and controversial simply because people care so deeply and want to do the right thing—but each one seems to think "the right thing" is the exact opposite of what someone else thinks. And church is those very same people coming together to help when one of them is in need. Invite everyone—and put on the appropriate clothes of caring and kindness.

*"Church"* is the new family who came to worship for the very first time, eager to learn more about how they could make a difference in their new community, who wanted to know what service projects the church sponsored so they could get involved immediately, and who wanted to know right away if there were people who would be alone for the holidays whom they could *invite* to share their Thanksgiving banquet.

*"Church"* is the huge pile of get-well cards with which we were flooded after my husband's heart attack at age forty-five on Christmas Day four years ago, and all the "fat free" recipes and exercise tips that people sent, along with the very sincere prayers, and the peaceful presence of the one who simply sat with me, in silence, those long hours, and the new pathways that opened to us in the months that followed to rich and wonderful new practices of meditation and centering prayer and healing prayer. *Come unto me, all of you!*

*"Church"* is the group of people who gather in an adult class every Sunday morning to study the problems in their city and what they might be able to do about them, who invited the candidates for public office to meet with them, who encouraged one of their number, a senior citizen, in fact "a little old lady in tennis shoes" (as she called herself) to run for *mayor* against the candidate sponsored by the movers, shakers, and developers in town, because they believed there was a better way, a more faithful, a more just way, to run that city. Invite everyone to *join* in working for the common good!

*"Church"* were all of our Congregational ancestors in the faith who left the comforts of home to go out to do and be and teach and preach the word of God to others—starting schools and colleges and churches for newly freed slaves all over the South just after the Civil War, taking ships to faraway places to spread the gospel in Angola, in Hawaii, and around the globe. Invite everyone to faith in Jesus Christ!

*"Church"* is Paula Bidle, daughter of Jim Bidle, our interim Conference minister before I arrived—Paula is serving now as a missionary of the United Church Board for World Ministries, among the native people of Guatemala, living in refugee camps in southern Mexico where

they fled for their lives from the violence of their own government. Reach out and touch everyone, everywhere, with God's love.

*"Church"* is where we learn how to pray, oh, maybe not so much in worship on Sunday morning, although that helps, but more in a small group at noon on Mondays, over a bag lunch, and several special times a year when we have a "silent retreat" with suggestions for how to pray and what to pray for and time set aside for *listening* prayer as well as speaking prayer. God invites everyone into a personal relationship in prayer!

*"Church"* is a woman dressed in a colorful African dashiki sitting alongside a man in a three-piece suit, sitting next to a kid in blue jeans and a T-shirt, each trying to appreciate and learn from each other a favorite song, so that all may be enriched, and so that all may give praise and glory to God! Come to the party, clothed in joy and gladness!

*"Church"* is where I experience being "born again," and again, and again, I seem to need it more often than most people, my memory must be short and my guilt quotient very high, but "church" is where I hear, again, the good news that God loves me, no matter what, that God promises to be with me, no matter what, and that God sends me out to share God's love with others. Y'all come!

*"Church"* is where I am challenged to confront my materialism, my negativism, my racism, my pessimism, my selfishness, my lack of faith. God invites everyone, and God expects me to respond accordingly!

*"Church"* is where people are willing to listen and learn from each other even about difficult, divisive issues on which they each initially think they hold diametrically opposing views. *"Church"* is the place our gay and lesbian brothers and sisters can, we hope, feel warmly welcomed. Invite everyone!

*"Church"* is a huge crowd of worshipers on Christmas Eve, all ages, lots of families with smiling children, in a growing area of town, where many new homes are going up, each person holding high a candle in hopeful anticipation. What a party, what a celebration!

*"Church"* is a very small number of people, mostly in their eighties, spread out sitting in separate pews in a rather large sanctuary, struggling with the question of how they can be faithful, and wondering what to do to *invite* the changing neighborhood into their hearts *and* into their

building, and asking themselves how much they will have to change the way they worship in order to invite others in.

"*Church*" was the scattered group of "confessing Christians" in pre-war Germany who vowed never to "confess" Hitler as their supreme ruler, but always to give their allegiance only to Christ. Some opened their attics to hide Jewish neighbors; others even participated in a plot to overthrow Hitler. "Many are called, but few are chosen."

"*Church*" is the feeling I got while holding a lighted candle inside a glass jar, and sitting quietly on a blanket on the cold ground at 3 A.M., singing softly, "Kum ba Yah," "Come by here, Lord," outside the prison where a person was about to be executed, praying for comfort and peace for the families of the victims, and for the family of the murderer, for the guards and for the other prisoners inside and for the jury and the lawyers and the police, and for the chaplain who was inside, and even praying for the people who were across the street drinking beer and laughing loudly and partying more wildly as the night wore on, all the while waiting in a vigil which, very oddly, felt very much like the time when I had waited at my own mother's bedside the night she died. What a strange party God has invited us to.

"*Church*" is sunrise on Easter morning, outside, knowing that God promises resurrection, that death does not have the last word, that new life is given once more, that every sunrise, in fact, is a mini-celebration of the resurrection, and every sunset is a call to thanksgiving for the blessings of the day. Come, everyone, praise the God of creation and resurrection!

"*Church*" is thanksgiving, and praise, and singing, and feasting, and caring and sharing and giving and loving, and hoping, and failing, and confessing, and being forgiven, and being called, and being sent out—again—and being inspired and being revived, and even being given a swift kick in the you-know-what, every once in a while. Church is where we are invited, *and* where we are asked to respond to the invitation!

"*Church*" is caring about decent jobs for everyone, a roof over their heads, an education for every child, good medical care for all, a world free from fear and hatred and tyranny and famine and war; *church is working to make that world come true*, one step at a time. Response!

"*Church*" is "us," not just "me;" "church" is "all of us," not just "the ones that look like me or act like me or think like me"; "church" is where they won't throw you out; "church" is where we don't have to agree all the time, we can agree to disagree in love; "church" is where I'm a little more willing to give up some of my opinions and listen to yours and maybe even be changed; "church" is *community*, not individuality; "church" is about giving, not hoarding; "church" is about our *need* to give and love and share; "church" is about rejoicing, about saying thanks no matter the circumstances, about not worrying about anything; but in everything, by prayer and supplication, making our requests known to God.

"*Church*" is about being made in the image of God; "church" is about giving thanks to God; "church" is about living always to the glory of God!

"*Church*" is about responding to the invitation to the party joyfully and willingly and wearing the clothes of goodness and love!

Praise be to God. Let us join our hearts in prayer:

Gracious and all-loving God, in every age you have called people to do your work, to show justice, to love mercy, to walk humbly with you. Empower your church, *(name of congregation)* United Church of Christ in *(name of town)*, and empower the Southwest Conference of the United Church of Christ, and your church around the world, to share in Christ's ministry as prophet, priest, and ruler, reconciling the world to your way and to your love, always giving thanks and praise to you. We pray in the name of Jesus Christ. Amen.

# T U R N T A B L E

DIANE (WOLFF) SNOWA

The dining table during my growing-up years was a table of purpose: eating. It was a table tucked into the corner of our small kitchen. It was a table marked more by silence than by sharing. It was a table where we three children knew, without a doubt, that children were to be seen and not heard. It was a table where, if anyone spoke, the voice would be my German-American father.

My mother was the preparer and the cleaner-upper. Plates were always cleaned of food as we were reminded of the starving children elsewhere in the world. That reminder was intended, I believe, not to inspire a compassion for others but rather to insist on obedience to the command of a parent.

Tables have a power for shaping lives.

In our little Lutheran church, the Table was denied to children. However, I remember well the sense of mystery, the sense of otherness, that I felt as I watched with the eye of a child the adults sharing the bread and drinking from the cup. I did not know who prepared that Table, nor who cleaned up afterward.

The church became a second home for me. Sunday school was a "must." I still hear my father's words: "Out on Saturday night, up on Sunday morning." A teenager in the 1950s did not disobey a father's insistence. However, my adolescent resistance does not define my allegiance to the church.

During my childhood, an adult choir member invited me to the church on Wednesday afternoons. She played the piano, and I sang hymns from our Lutheran hymnal. I often wonder if I had been for her the daughter she had never had. Miss Katie sang in the choir. She had the most off-key voice I had ever heard. Her determination was remarkable. More remarkable was the acceptance and encouragement she received at church. She regularly soloed, flat and determined. My subconscious perceived that the church is the second home for many. Even off-key singers are respected, received, encouraged, and loved sacrificially.

College and career ensued. Marriage and childbearing followed. Churchgoing remained the constant. Then, broken covenants and a near-death experience. Churchgoing remained the constant.

During my thirty-something years, I realized that hymns nurture me, that prayers nurture me, the sense of belonging nurtures me, that the Table of the Transcendent nurtures me. I felt a confidence I had not felt earlier.

Perhaps it was that confidence that allowed the tumultuous 1970s to quicken within me a relationship with our broken world. I realized that respect, reception, acceptance, encouragement, and sacrificial love are not extended to all persons, even in the church. Within me a restlessness rumbled. Churchgoing no longer answered my questions. I withdrew.

Gracefully, however, the theological pause became the Spirit's playground. The restlessness within found its rest, not in church, but in God, a God who demands justice, a God who weeps with me, a God of undeniable mystery.

By the mid-1970s I was reading Tillich, Niebuhr, Bultmann, and Moltmann. By the late 1970s, I had to do something! I needed a place beyond home and career. I returned to church. I chaired committees, wrote liturgy, sang in the choir; and then, oops, when I was ready, I was denied a leadership position because a male was being primed for it. I felt anger!

With my then thirteen-year-old son, I volunteered a year of our lives to the Institute for Cultural Affairs, the social justice arm of the Ecumenical Institute based in Chicago. They sent us to rural Brazil to work in a newly initiated Human Development Project. Of course, I had never seen such poverty. I had never been in a culture other than white and European.

The experience had two prongs. First, in the village I worked with the other ICA staff members. This was a wonderful shared-gifts experience quite different from teaching in a public high school classroom. We enabled the villagers to take responsibility for the quality of life in the village. A preschool was established and teachers trained. An elementary after-school program was initiated and coordinators trained. A health care program taught villagers to weigh babies, to monitor infant progress, to be aware of their own wellness habits, to treat wounds (like machete slashes) with tourniquets, and to vary their diets. Yes, we introduced them to gardening and to preparing and eating vegetables— an interesting phenomenon for people who have no teeth.

Using materials available from the national program, I taught Portuguese language skills to the adults. The thrill, though, was my teaching any of the children who desired how to speak English. My personal bias is that, by one's learning to speak another language, the concept of possibility is expanded beyond imagination. I wanted these children, who had been born into the web of poverty, to have as many images, as much motivation, as much will as possible to break the web.

In an effort to create a caretaker cadre, I trained six youth in health and hygiene skills. One afternoon, I attempted to demonstrate tourniquets to stop the bleeding from knife wounds and machete slashings. When I paired the girls so they could practice applying tourniquets, one girl appeared horrified. She could not touch the *preto*.

Her partner was the darkest Brazilian in my group, whose family, I learned, all deeply colored, were shunned by the other villagers. My black/white lens was shattered. I learned for the first time that people of color have their own biases.

Hearing the girls' descriptions, I suspended the lesson on tourniquets. There was more serious bleeding that needed remedy. I remember approaching the very dark body at our table. I took her hands in mine. I massaged her arms to the shoulders and bent to kiss her forehead.

Using my inferior Portuguese language skills, but aided by necessary and universal body language, I taught that underneath the skin, which has different shades throughout the world, we all have a heart that holds the same love, a mind that can hold "mucho" information, and a soul that is bathed by an incredible and awesome God.

The girls became animated by their new understanding. Although I could not understand the words that filled the room, I rejoiced in the spirit as the girls leaned across the table toward the shunned one to touch her, to embrace her, to receive her.

Shortly thereafter, the girl's mother gave birth to a robust son. What a joy it was to see "my girls" visiting that bamboo shack, holding that baby and embracing new life in more ways than one.

Returning to the United States, I was greeted by my school district who penalized me a year's salary increase in response to my leaving for the year; by my mother who wanted to punish me for taking her grandson away from her for a year; and by my son's profound depression in finding no way to process what he had experienced. It was a scary time!

Prayer took on greater depth and greater heights. I sensed a call to ordained ministry. A woman. A middle-aged woman. A divorced single-parent woman. When I shared this sensed call with my minister, he replied, "Diane, I can see you in business!" and regretfully I yielded to the lack of affirmation.

By 1983, a coercive compulsion pushed me toward seminary. I resigned from teaching, withdrew my funds from the retirement system, sought student loans, and found two part-time jobs. Tuition, at least for a year, appeared satisfied, based on the promise of a large scholarship from the seminary. In late July, I received notice that the scholarship had been offered to another candidate. I was devastated.

I drove to the seminary and sought the director of admissions. He invited me to sit across from him at the table in his office. I showed him the letter I had received and asked, "How can this be? You led me to believe I would receive the scholarship." He replied, "Sell your house!"

Numbed by betrayal, I entered seminary, a setting where women were received but seldom respected, rarely encouraged, and certainly not loved. How does one sing the Lord's song in a strange land?

The answer came as an invitation to sing with an ecumenical choir embarking on a peace mission to Poland, a country still behind the Iron

Curtain. The contradiction was my lack of money. I had withdrawn all my money from the teacher retirement program; I had emptied my savings account; I had a student loan; I was working two part-time jobs; and I had rented out a room in my home. How on earth could I finance a trip to Poland?

Inspired by a dream, I sat at my dining room table and wrote to everyone on my Christmas card list, to selected college and seminary friends, and to family. I shared my gratitude for the invitation and for my gifts of voice and time. I invited my friends to share the ministry of song by sharing their gifts of money. In return, for any who could be in St. Louis during September, there would be a gathering at my home, when I would share the experience with them. Every day, I prayed, and how passionately I imaged the $1975 I needed so desperately.

Checks began to come. Two were larger than $50; the majority were written for $10 and $20, even a few $5s. When the total reached $1975, the checks stopped! Right on the button: $1975. I learned a very valuable lesson about the abundance of God: Never put a cap on a request. I think I may have limited God's outpouring. My joy overflowed. The trip remains one of those sacred memories: two thousand Poles walking across their country to view the famous "Charna Madonna," our singing in cathedrals, palaces, and an abandoned salt mine where prisoners had been held during the Nazi years; a day at Auschwitz, my hugging a Polish sister who lived and hoped for a day of liberation. I would never be the same person as the one who had embarked on the experience.

Returning to the States, I was assigned a student pastorate, a small rural United Church of Christ congregation that had been without a pastor for two years. I was now a senior, searching for the call that would lead to ordination. I circulated my profile in New York State, Pennsylvania, Michigan, and Wisconsin. I wanted North, especially when I heard the congregational leaders frequently asserting, "We don't want a woman."

At the end of my student assignment and near graduation from seminary, this rural Missouri church extended a call to me. I didn't want it. There had to be more comfort, more reward, more money, more possibility elsewhere. I talked with Conference ministers from the geographies I had chosen. Without delay, God entered the discussion; and consequently, I accepted the call and was ordained in the United Church of Christ in eastern Missouri.

For over three years, I struggled with the congregation's distrust, their resisting Bible study with new questions, their resisting non-gender language, their resisting contemporary hymns, their resisting emerging female lay leadership, and their allegiance to male leadership that rebelled against expanded images of God. We are talking 1988 c.e. The most stalwart leader and his family left the church. I was blamed, but refused the "honor." Gradually, the congregation committed themselves to a building program. The foundation of a sixty-by-eighty-foot education building was poured; the water and electric conduits were installed; the ten-year flat line was replaced with a ten-year vision. My time with them was fulfilled.

My serving in that rural setting held many surprises. Like the day I drove the dirt road leading to the church nestled among forty acres to meet my confirmation student. He and his dad cautioned me to slow down my '67 Camaro convertible. (Members had already dubbed me "the hot-rod pastor.") As I left my car, seventeen wild turkeys emerged from the clump of trees and took flight. We counted them, and I was filled with awe at the power of the creation.

Another lesson in rural living came after a worship service one Sunday. Now, I had cautioned this congregation that I was a "city girl," and their responsibility was to teach me "how to be rural." The lessons began that Sunday morning. As I opened the doors to prepare for the congregation's exit, there they were—a cow and a bull copulating in the field that lay between the church building and the road. My citified biases eased, and I tacitly blessed their union and turned my attention to the human flock.

The next call was to a historic church in a river bluff community. The treasury was near depletion. The congregation was resigned to changing times that were destroying their farming community. A glass blower had taken over the garage that had been the setting for farm machinery repair. Quilters, crafters, and artists were moving into abandoned homesteads. The wineries were attracting great numbers of tourists. The traditional families were losing their "home."

The village had no restaurants spacious enough to accommodate large groups of tourists; a call to creative ministry took root. This lovely church in a pastoral setting had a spacious fellowship hall, a modern kitchen, plus the former detached kitchen. The widows of the congregation responded to a suggestion for a ministry of hospitality. Tourism was taking hold in this Missouri River Bluff community; and at the church, home-style fried chicken and roast beef dinners were offered at the fellowship hall. Gradually, as the enthusiasm of the women soared, the male doubt waned—aided by the growing figures in the church treasury. One day, we signed our fourteenth contract with a tour bus company.

Another three-year call had been fulfilled. Without minimizing the pain of initial rebuke and continued doubt, I became convinced that ministry, even for a sixty-year-old female, was fun!

Two of my fondest memories are with that church. I was not only the pastor but also the choir director. We were singing "Lord of the Dance" as the recessional. I suggested that the choir literally dance as they recess. The younger members received the idea with consenting snickers; the oldest, most quiet, most shy one shook her head. But, on Sunday morning, as the choir recessed, there was Alma, joining the others—doing a 360-degree turn, on her toes, and grinning ear to ear.

The other memory is more personal. While serving this church, I started dating another UCC minister, and we decided to marry. The congregation gave me no choice as to where; the reception was theirs to design. We had a celebration that overflowed not only with food and drink but also with a joy so profound that even today, ten years later, when I return to the river's bluff for a visit, tears of joy flow liberally from all of our hearts.

During these two local-church pastorates, which were each part-time positions, I also served as the first Protestant chaplain in a hospital associated with the Roman Catholic Church. The pastoral care department included one priest and two nuns. The struggle with ecumenicity was filled with snags.

For example, the mass for the families who had lost loved ones to death included Holy Communion only for the Catholic families. Priests, at that time, were under orders to serve the eucharist only to Catholics. The bulletin included the statement: "While the Catholics celebrate the Holy Eucharist, let us pray for the day when all Christians might commune together." Transforming the service to include all families took many, many months and much soul searching. Finally, the priest, the nuns, and I reached a consensus on language that could be interpreted to include all persons while the bulletin clearly stated "during the Holy Eucharist, let us pray for the day when all Christians will commune together." The priest was protected, and Catholics and Protestants approached the Table together.

At the hospital, the intricacies of ecumenicity and the demands of evaluating tradition became real for me as I worked with the pastoral care department head, an older well-meaning nun. At one point, she asked that I influence people to call me "Chaplain" rather than "Pastor" since my "ordination is not a requirement for the position." I sensed immediately that at least one part of her motivation was that, in her tradition, she could not be ordained. I think it was painful for her to work with a woman who was ordained. In time, the conversations ended when I asked if the priest needed to give up his "Father" since that was the title of his ordination just as "Pastor" or "Reverend" was for me.

Within a year of our marriage, my husband received a call to a staff position in his home state. Reluctantly, I accompanied him to his call in southeastern Virginia—a different cultural more and very different roles for the genders. I immediately met a brick wall of resistance, impenetrable for a midwesterner whose first twenty-five years had been in New York. "Yankee, go home," was the greeting at Association clergy meetings.

Fortunately, there were loose bricks in the wall.

I was invited by two clergymen to "guest" preach from the pulpit in the churches they were serving. My husband's position was the lever that opened the door. I wrestled with the ambiguities that I felt allowing my husband's position to place me in a pulpit. However, I swallowed hard and yielded. I missed preaching so deeply, and only later realized the value of my yielding. In those churches, I was the first woman ever to have been granted permission to preach. One woman shared with a mutual friend, "I had to clench my fist and grit my teeth. Women just shouldn't preach!" Today, not only women but also clergy of color are preaching from these pulpits.

With the wonderful urging of a retired minister in the Association, I was asked to fill an interim position at a local church. He advocated for my being named, and reluctantly, the congregation accepted a woman. However, immersed in my enthusiasm for having a position and with greater enthusiasm for the tremendous laity participation in ministry that was emerging, especially among the women of the congregation, I was blind to the undermining that was being enacted by two male parishioners in leadership positions. Suddenly, a minister from out-of-state was called, and I was out. The chaos that resulted in that congregation was church life at its worst.

Without a call to a church, I returned reluctantly to teaching. The local community college needed an English instructor, and I slipped into the vacancy. I taught developmental English (reading and writing skills) to high school graduates whose skills were deficient for college success. I hated being kept out of ministry!

During that time, the Conference minister visited our geography and stayed in our home. As we shared at the breakfast table one morning the difficulty clergywomen were having with call, I suggested the issue might be a justice issue. I shared my experience.

My husband and I had discussed the reality that if I were to have a congregation, the call would have to come from elsewhere, preferably within the Conference but outside our Association. I had learned of an interim opening within four hours of our home, a part-time call that would have enabled me to be home two to two-and-a-half days a week. I alerted the Conference officials of my desire to serve that congregation. A retired male minister, however, was slipped into the slot.

As the Conference minister sat at our table, I brought up my concern. Clergywomen often serve interim positions in order to have at least a short-term experience in their calls from God. I asked, "Is it not a justice issue that you assign to these openings males who are retired, who do not need the experience, who do not need the money?"

Throwing his arms into the air, he replied, "But they're good!" Damn! And I had thought I was!

After two years of no opportunity to serve a church, I met the regional minister of the Virginia Christian (Disciples of Christ) Church. Perhaps out of desperation, but certainly enabled by the advocacy of the Virginia DOC Women's Fellowship, he invited me to fill an interim position with the Disciples. That first call led to a second, and I not only was able to practice ordained spiritual leadership but also identified what was probably the call God had had in mind all along. My previous teacher/counselor career, my personal gifts, my disposition, my adaptability to change, all had found their place—focused interim ministry in the local church.

As I now look back, I recall my mountaintop experience in ministry. It occurred during the second interim pastorate for the Disciples, 1999–2000. The setting was a small historic church; it was a ministry-marriage every clergy person should experience. After the initial clarification of values and reasons for their former ministry having gone awry, my style and theirs erupted into thirteen glorious months of initiating new programs, strengthening existing programs, enabling new leadership, and offering three worship services: 8:30 A.M., 11:00 A.M., and 6:00 P.M. each Sunday. Twenty-one converts were led to the Baptismal pool, and twenty-six names were added to the membership roster. Those thirteen months continue to nurture me! I cannot explain fully the profound spiritual impact of a wounded healer being at the Table every Sunday. There is a balm in Gilead!

However, a dynamic occurred in this church that many clergywomen experience sooner or later during these pioneering days. Traditionally, each congregation has a woman or a cadre of women who care for the male pastor. The role is self-imposed, appreciated, and it is defining. The relationship often entails homemade goodies for the pastor and *his* family. It often means special smiles and affirming words. The woman's identity is informed by her understanding of her role in the church. When a clergywoman enters the church for the first time, this role is deposed. (Women usually do not serve women.) Therefore, there is a role loss, an identity loss, and the female clergy finds it very difficult to establish meaningful relationship with this former "first lady (ladies) of the church." The loss of sisterhood is painful.

Today, I am serving as interim minister in a UCC church in which a slight majority of the membership was intentionally desirous of having a clergywoman. A few families left the church stating that women should not be pastors. However, what thrills me is that UCC members, who have been connected to the openness and straightforwardness of the UCC but have been reluctant to speak, are finding their voices. Hearing their new song is healing salve to the pain the past wrought.

As I reflect on these dozen years of ordained ministry, I glory in God's steadfastness even when I was prone to give up. The cost and the joy of faithful discipleship are so entwined, so intermingled, like the blood and the water that flowed from the pierced side of the crucified Christ. In closing, I want to recall a sermon I preached in 1999 from the Lucan text, chapter 24:13–35, the Emmaus road story.

After reading the text and reiterating the story, I asked the congregation, "What have we learned about disciples this morning? What have we learned about ourselves?" I went on:

> The two disciples were experiencing the events in life very differently from the way they would have preferred. They HAD HOPED this Jesus would redeem. But it had not happened the way they had envisioned; they were sad. They were disheartened. There is no evidence of hope. There is no thought of possibility. There is no consideration of a God who perhaps is at work, living and loving, even in the midst of tragedy and tomb. No, it did not happen the way they thought it would happen, and so it is not happening at all.
>
> MOREOVER—that is Luke's word, not mine—moreover, some of the women of our group had visited the tomb. They came back and told us they had seen the angels and had heard these angels say, "He is alive."
>
> The disciples had heard the good news. They did not believe. Why should they? Women aren't believable. Their word is suspect. They belong on the sidelines, in the back of the temple, shouldn't teach, shouldn't preach, shouldn't be proclaiming the good news. Their news can't teach us—and it didn't.
>
> Luke continues, even when some of our men returned to the tomb, maybe they wanted to believe the women, maybe these had heard Jesus' teachings and watched his behavior that made equals of women—these men returned, but they didn't see anything.
>
> Disciples are hardheaded, aren't they? If things are not as we want them, we remain steadfast in what was! What is it that keeps us from believing the good news as it comes to us, even as it comes to us from those we want to keep on the sidelines? What is it that feeds our arrogance? We know the answer. It is our sin; our separation from our God.
>
> When I donated a year to serve among the poor in Brazil, I heard faith stories so profound from among the "least of these."

I witnessed a faith that is so profound among those who do not
have all the things, all the stuff, that help to erode faith. From
those who lived in mud and bamboo huts, who eat wormy rice
and beans every day, who live with no electricity, and no chance
to learn to read and write, I learned the meaning of faith. From
people of color who live down there, in South America, I heard
the good news of Jesus Christ, alive, liberating, and redeeming.

When I traveled to war-torn Angola on the continent of
Africa two years ago, I heard faith stories so profound among
"the least of these." I witnessed a faith so profound among those
who do not have all the things, all the stuff, that help to erode
faith. From those who live among seventeen million landmines
buried in their soil, who live with their homes, their schools,
their hospitals, leveled by warfare, I heard the good news of
Jesus Christ, alive, liberating, and redeeming.

When I served on a pastoral care team for persons with
AIDS, I heard faith stories from among the "least of these."
From those who live with emaciated bodies, eaten away by disease with no hope of recovery, I learned the meaning of faith.
From those who had been rejected from family, from home,
from employment, from community, from church because of
sexual orientation or drug addiction, I witnessed the profundi-
ty of faith. I heard the good news of Jesus Christ, alive, liberating, and redeeming.

As a woman of middle class America, I have met the living
and liberating and redeeming Christ—not in the schools where
I could not receive the math award because boys should win the
math awards, not in the church where I could not hold office
because officers should be men; but I met the Christ at the
empty tomb where Jesus could not and cannot be contained.

What is it that feeds our arrogance that keeps others outside? More important, what is it that takes that arrogance away?

On that day, when the disciples could not believe the experiences of another, the stranger stayed with them, went with
them to the table, and broke bread. Only then could they
remember: "Were our hearts not burning within us while he was

talking with us on the road, while he was opening the scriptures to us? Were not our hearts burning, our arrogance cleansed?"

Friends, disciples, it is only at the Table where our sin is embraced, our arrogance embraced, our blindness embraced, our deafness embraced, our hearts set on fire. Only at the table in the breaking of the bread can we break forth from all that holds us to the prejudices of the past. Only at the Table in the breaking of the bread is it made known that for the whole world he died and was raised again. Only from the Table can we go to those we want to ignore. Only from the Table can we go and proclaim, "He is risen, Savior, Liberator, and Redeemer." Only from the Table, can we go and live risen lives, lives led by hearts set on fire by the resurrection power of a living and loving, liberating and redeeming God. Amen.

Last month on World Communion Sunday, an interesting thing happened at the Table. I had invited a Muslim colleague and friend to share a message with the congregation I am serving. He traced his journey that began in a family belonging to the Baptist Church, continued through Roman Catholic schools, and lodges now in a call to Islam as a messenger of reconciliation. He has served our country as a Muslim chaplain in the U.S. military and is now pursuing his doctorate to become a professor of Islamic history.

He shared images of Allah and the practices of prayer in Muslim life. He alluded frequently to the awe he, a Muslim, was feeling having been invited to a Christian worship service on World Communion Sunday.

Following the message, I invited us all to the Table, to God's Table, a foretaste of the feast that is to come, to a Table of reconciliation. Together, Christians and a Muslim ate the bread of a broken world and drank from the cup of grace poured out and calling us all to lives liberated and redeemed, saved and marked with the commandment to love friend and foe, neighbor and stranger.

Today, I allude frequently to the presence of a God who loves without boundary, who redeems the world, who liberates the children, and who reconciles the creation. For me, that is table talk, and tables do have a power for shaping lives.

# PRAYER FOR THE LAST SUNDAY OF EASTER

### May 15, 1983

DIANE (WOLFF) SNOWA

Heavenly One, the Giver, Sustainer and Taker of all that we are, all that we do, and all that we know: our hearts are filled with thanksgiving this morning for the gift of Life and the promise of rebirth, for the presence of Spring color, for the rebirth of the natural world and for the resurrection of all that seems dead. You have colored your world, Lord, and we pray that you color and recolor us.

Color us purple, Lord,
    so that we might feel the passion of thy Son, Jesus Christ.
Let us wear that purple robe
beneath the crown of thorns.
Let us hear the pleading of the poor,
        the howling of the hungry,
        the crying of the naked,
        the wailing of the imprisoned,
        the laughter of the oppressors.

Then, Lord, color us orange
   so that we might have our wild restlessness
transformed to energy that serves an agonized world.
Yes, Lord, color us orange
so that we
          might risk
          might somehow redress
          the injustices that plague the planet Ours.

Color us red, Lord,
   so that the blood of Christ
might flow through our lives and
into all the Samarias we choose to travel.
Color us red, Lord,
so that you and
          Jesus and
          each of us
          might be One—
          the formula that allows one to love and honor every
          living thing on this earth.

Color us green, Lord,
   so that we might know
the greenness of your healing powers nested within us;
green, Lord, the color of rebirth
so that every deathly and dreadful atom of our beings
might be resurrected
          into life and wholeness,
          into love and forgiveness,
          into courage and confidence
   so that the peace in our God-center
might propel us to walk
          the threatening and
          dangerous and
          unpopular paths of your Will.

Color us white, Lord,
    so that the purity of your purpose
might be so untainted by earthly values.
Color us white, Lord,
so that the colors of your spectrum
might be reflected into this universe and universes beyond.

And finally, Lord, color us black.
    Color us that beautiful and awesome black
    so that we
    might absorb your rainbow
    and stand in the midst
    of the mysteries not yet revealed,
    and scream, "I believe. I believe!"

Yes, Lord, wash away the veneer,
    this lousy veneer, Lord.
We're so tired of being so phony,
        so artificial,
        so comfortable,
        so careful.

    Wash away this veneer, color us, Lord,
so that the only covenant is with You
        The God that is Creator
        The God that is Community,
        The God that is Continual,
        The God that is the Caller for Justice.

Wash away the veneer, dear Lord,
    So that we might be
        might do
            might know
                All that is You.

In the name of Jesus Christ. Amen.

# CONTRIBUTORS

Robin J. Townsley Arcus is an ordained UCC minister acting as supply; she is also a regular contributor to the regional nonfiction magazine *The Urban Hiker.*

Dora M. Atlas came to the United Church of Christ from AME Zion. After retirement from pastoral ministry, she founded Our Daily Bread, a hunger ministry in Asheboro, North Carolina, and remains actively involved at age eighty-three.

Kaye W. Crawford, the founding minister of Hillsborough United Church of Christ in Hillsborough, North Carolina, has served as its pastor for fourteen years. She is entering semi-retirement in 2004 and plans to write and to lead workshops and retreats.

For nearly forty years, Yvonne V. Delk has been a strong ally in the fight for human and civil rights for people of color, children, and the poor. From 1990 to 1998, she served as the executive director of Community Renewal Society, a faith-based Chicago metropolitan area agency that works to empower people to dismantle racism and poverty. Before that, she served as executive director of the United Church of Christ's Office of Church in Society. In 1974, she became the first African American woman to be ordained in the United Church of Christ.

Jill R. Edens has been, since 1979, copastor with her husband of United Church of Chapel Hill, North Carolina. United Church is a multiethnic, multicultural Open and Affirming church and shares its space with Iglesia Unida de Cristo and the Ismaili Community (Islam).

Mary Emma Evans was the first African American woman to pastor a church in the Eastern North Carolina Association of the United Church of Christ.

**Sallye Hardy** is an ordained minister in the United Church of Christ. Her passion is pastoral care of women and children. She can be reached at hardys@alumni .duke.edu.

**Lynne Hinton** has served as the pastor of two congregations in the Southern Conference. She is the author of six books including *Friendship Cake* (HarperSan Francisco, 2000) and *The Last Odd Day* (HarperSan Francisco, 2004). Currently, she lives in Santa Fe, New Mexico. She can be reached at Lynbob2677@aol.com.

**Nancy Peeler Keppel** is a UCC Commissioned Minister. In 1974, she initiated the Southern Conference Women in Church and Society Task Force. A political and social activist, she is a reality therapist and cofounder of CLAY: Clergy and Laity Together in Ministry. She can be reached at NPKep@aol.com.

**Denise Cumbee Long** is the executive director of NC LEAF, the North Carolina Legal Education Assistance Foundation, and a Program Associate with the North Carolina Council of Churches. She lives in Raleigh, North Carolina, with her husband, two mostly grown children, and two dogs.

**Ann H. McLaughlin** is a retired pastoral counselor living in Raleigh, North Carolina.

**Maria Palmer** is the founding pastor of Iglesia Unida de Cristo in Chapel Hill, North Carolina. She is a post-doctoral Rockefeller Fellow at UNC-Chapel Hill and has served on the North Carolina State Board of Education since 1999.

**Julie Peeples** has served in staff and chaplaincy positions in Massachusetts, Pennsylvania, and Georgia, and is currently pastor of Congregational UCC, Greensboro, North Carolina.

**Cally Rogers-Witte** is the Conference Minister of the Southwest Conference of the United Church of Christ. Before that she was pastor of Community UCC in Raleigh, North Carolina, for almost eighteen years.

**Diane (Wolff) Snowa** is now "retired" but sharing ministry with her husband at historic St. John's UCC in Louisville, Kentucky. Pastor Diane served two churches in Missouri Conference UCC, three churches in Southern Conference (Virginia) UCC, and two churches in Virginia Disciples of Christ. Her forte has been focused interim ministry. Concurrent with all local church ministries, she served as a part-time chaplain at the local hospitals in Missouri and Virginia.